RUNE BEGINNERS

The Comprehensive Guide to the Reading and Meaning of Elder Futhark Runes. Explore the Magical Spells, Rituals, and Symbols of Norse Magic.

JÖRMUNDUR HJARTARSON
ZED&KEI PUBLICATIONS

© Copyright 2024 by Jörmundur Hjartarson
Zed&Kei Publications
All rights reserved.

This document is geared towards providing exact and reliable information in regards to the topic and issue covered. The publication is sold with the idea that the publisher is not required to render accounting, officially permitted, or otherwise, qualified services. If advice is necessary, legal or professional, a practiced individual in the profession should be ordered.

From a Declaration of Principles which was accepted and approved equally by a Committee of the American Bar Association and a Committee of Publishers and Associations.

In no way is it legal to reproduce, duplicate, or transmit any part of this document in either electronic means or printed format. Recording of this publication is strictly prohibited and any storage of this document is not allowed unless with written permission from the publisher. All rights reserved.

The information provided herein is stated to be truthful and consistent, in that any liability, in terms of inattention or otherwise, by any usage or abuse of any policies, processes, or directions contained within is the solitary and utter responsibility of the recipient reader. Under no circumstances will any legal responsibility or blame be held against the publisher for any reparation, damages, or monetary loss due to the information herein, either directly or indirectly.

Respective authors own all copyrights not held by the publisher.

The information herein is offered for informational purposes solely and is universal as so. The presentation of the information is without a contract or any type of guarantee assurance.

The trademarks that are used are without any consent, and the publication of the trademark is without permission or backing by the trademark owner. All trademarks and brands within this book are for clarifying purposes only and are owned by the owners themselves, not affiliated with this document.

TABLE OF CONTENTS

INTRODUCTION 1

01
THE NORDIC PEOPLE 4
THE VIKINGS 5
THE NORSE RELIGION 8

02
THE ORIGIN OF THE WORLD 13
THE BIRTH OF THE GODS 16
THE CREATION OF HUMANS 16

03
THE NORSE PANTHEON 18
THE AESIR 19
THE VANIR 27
MYTHICAL CREATURES 31

04
NORSE RELIGIOUS PRACTICES 35
NORSE FESTIVALS 38
RITUALS AND SPELLS 46
RITES OF PASSAGE 48
NORSE RELIGION IN MODERN PRACTICES 55

05

MODERN NORSE RELIGION 56
- ASATRU 56
- CORE TEACHINGS OF MODERN ASATRU PRACTICES 58
- BELIEFS 63
- THE NINE NOBLE VIRTUES OF ASATRU 65
- INTERACTING WITH ASATRU COMMUNITIES 70
- HEATHENRY 71

06

NORSE PAGANISM 74
- PAGAN MORALITY AND ETHICS 75
- THE BLOT 76
- THE SUMBLE 77
- PROFESSION 80
- TALISMANS 81
- CREATING A TALISMAN 81
- ALTARS 86
- INDOOR ALTARS 87
- OUTDOOR ALTARS 88

07

THE RUNES 90
- THE HISTORY OF RUNES 90
- USING RUNES 93
- THE RUNIC ALPHABET 96

08

FUNDAMENTALS OF DIVINATION 106
- RUNES IN DIVINATION 106
- CHOOSING RUNES 111

CASTING RUNES	112
INTERPRETING RUNES	114
MEDITATION CAN HELP IN READINGS	115
NORSE MAGIC OVER TIME	118

09
AETTIR ... 120
THE AETT OF FREYR	122
THE AETT OF HAGAL OR HEIMDALL	124
THE AETT OF TYR	132
ODIN'S RUNE	141

10
RUNES TIPS AND SECRETS ... 148
CREATING A SET OF RUNES	148
SUITABLE MATERIALS	154
CHOOSING COLORS	156
CONTAINERS FOR RUNES	157
THE READING CLOTH	158

11
PRESERVING THE RUNES ... 160
CLEANSING THE RUNES	160
CONSECRATING THE RUNES	161
EMPOWERING THE RUNES	164
RECHARGING THE RUNES	165
CREATING A SACRED SPACE	166
PREPARING FOR CASTING	167

12
READING THE RUNES ... 169
READING TECHNIQUES	169

| WRITING WITH RUNES | 171 |

13
LAYOUT FOR READING — 175

14
COSMOLOGY AND NUMEROLOGY — 194
| COSMOLOGY | 194 |
| NUMEROLOGY | 200 |

15
THE POEMS OF THE GODS — 203
THE EDDAS	203
POETIC EDDA	203
PROSE EDDA	205
MAGIC AND POETRY	207
RUNE POEMS	209
CONCLUSIONS	210

INTRODUCTION

Norse magic encompasses a set of practices that can have a great impact on a person's life. It can range from simple spells to intricate rituals involving runes and pagan beliefs. Undoubtedly, magic provides individuals with purpose and substance, offering a means to explore one's spiritual side and navigate the mystical realm. It also serves as a tool for self-discovery and understanding one's inner self. Although it is a free-for-all activity, it remains highly unique and meaningful. However, mastering with magic is no easy feat, as numerous factors must be aligned for it to be harnessed effectively. Although many individuals have the potential to harness its power, only a select few succeed. The key lies in awakening and channeling one's inner power while seeking the guidance of the gods. With time and understanding, one's magical abilities will gradually reveal themselves. Norse magic is strongly influenced by the concept of destiny. Its practitioners see it as a means of examining and potentially exercising control over one's fate, rather than altering it. In addition, Norse magic is devoted to the idea of manifesting wishes through written symbols or spoken words that represent them. This manifestation process is closely related to the practice of Galdr, with runes serving as a key component. Although we may begin as novices, it is always the best time to embrace the power of Norse magic in our lives. Runes, an ancient and enigmatic alphabet, are a significant medium for casting spells and for divination. Often considered sacred elements, they were predominantly found in warriors' amulets and armor. Runes play a vital role in Norse religion and spirituality, offering countless possibilities for use even in contemporary times. They possess a seductive quality due to their mystical and spiritual nature. The advice is simple: experiment with runes with a desire to discover their power. The practice of Norse magic emphasizes the duality of good and evil, positive and negative forces. The Norse believed that all elements of the universe were imbued with life and harnessed the energy flowing through them to enhance their well-being. This life force, known as "líf" in Norse magical circles, draws inspiration from mythology and seeks to appease the gods and goddesses of that era. Establishing contact with these divine beings was considered essential to gain their favor and avoid provoking their wrath. The ancient Norse regarded the elements of nature as divine entities, using earth, air, fire, water and plants as primary channels for their magical practices. Before engaging in any magical endeavor, they constantly consulted these elements, recognizing their inherent vitality and considering themselves as part of this living world. To perform spells, the Norse primarily used runes, a fundamental means of connecting with deities and fate. Repetition of these spells was often necessary to achieve the desired results. Runes served a multitude of purposes within the ancient Norse magical system. They facilitated communication with spiritual beings by casting spells, bestowing blessings and curses, and obtaining signs from other realms. Practitioners of Norse magic firmly believe in the interconnectedness of the two worlds. In addition to invoking and communicating with spirits, many individuals throughout history have explored Norse magic to gain information about their future or life in general. Now let's begin this extraordinary adventure!

01
THE NORDIC PEOPLE

The term "Norsemen" refers to the Nordic peoples residing in the North Atlantic region, which includes present-day Scandinavia (Norway, Denmark, Sweden) and Iceland. Before the Viking Age, these peoples spoke an ancient language with Germanic and Indo-European origins. From the 8th century onward, historical evidence reveals the introduction of established practices and beliefs that coincide with the period of foreign influences. This indicates a form of regulated paganism, so to speak. Their society lacked a strong literary tradition, so understanding their way of life requires an understanding of their oral tradition, as seen in early runic inscriptions and later sagas and poems. Stories were told, and their interpretations were subject to individual understanding. The Norse engaged primarily in agriculture, fishing, and trade, and it is important to recognize that their way of life went beyond the raids and conquests recounted in many tales. Their connection with their mythologies and magical rituals was deeply rooted in their daily existence. It can be called a unified and intricate civilization.

THE VIKINGS

The Vikings came from Sweden, Norway and Denmark long before these regions were officially recognized as independent countries. Mainly farmers and fishermen, the Vikings lived in villages under the rule of tribal chiefs or clan leaders. Their society was not highly urbanized; only a few towns existed. These tribal leaders were often engaged in territorial disputes, using their formidable armies and bands of warriors. The reasons behind the Vikings' decision to leave their homeland and undertake sea raids are uncertain, but historians propose a couple of theories. Political instability, resulting from frequent clan clashes, may have spurred their expansion. Another possible factor is localized overpopulation, which would have led to smaller land holdings that could no longer support all family members. In addition, during the 7th and 8th centuries, the Vikings made significant advances in shipbuilding, incorporating sails and modifying their ships to support longer voyages. These highly maneuverable long ships enabled them to cross the North Sea and land on new shores. Considering the progress of navigation, the difficult socioeconomic circumstances of the Vikings at that time, and the adventurous nature of a people with a warrior spirit, it is not difficult to understand why they eventually chose to raid the shores of Europe. The first documented Viking raid was in 793, when a monastery in Lindisfarne, England, was looted for its valuable religious artifacts. However, it is unlikely that this incident marked the first time the Vikings attacked England. Evidence suggests that English coastal villages had already begun organizing defenses against sea attacks as early as the 8th century, indicating earlier Viking raids or invasion attempts. Medieval English documents often referred to the Vikings as "maritime pagans" because of their preference for targeting sacred sites, which were often populated by unarmed individuals and contained valuable treasures. Therefore, it is understandable why the Vikings took advantage of such opportunities.

The term "Viking," derived from the ancient Scandinavian word "vikingir" (pirate) or "vik" (bay), became widely used toward the end of the Viking Age. Europeans, unlucky enough to face their own aggression, commonly referred to Scandinavian warriors as "Dani" (inhabitants of Denmark), "Norsemen" (Northmen) or simply "Pagans" (heathens). Beginning in 793, Viking bands, composed of slaves, servants and young adventurers led by chieftains, continued to attack England and surrounding regions, particularly Scotland, Ireland and France. In addition, accounts from the last years of the Viking Age mention attacks or sightings of Vikings in the Iberian Peninsula, Ukraine, Russia, and even the Byzantine Empire. Initially, raids were relatively small-scale, involving only a few ships, and the Vikings gladly returned home once they had acquired sufficient booty or encountered strong resistance. However, beginning in the 1850s, the Vikings began to increase the scope and organization of their raids, establishing bases in newly conquered territories and gaining dominance over neighboring islands.

During the Bronze Age, the Celts and Vikings were the predominant groups in the northern regions. It was inevitable that these two cultures would influence each other. The Celts inhabited northern England, Scotland and Ireland, extending as far as northern Italy and Spain. Some theories suggest a genetic connection between Vikings and Celts because of their similar languages and cultures. However, the truth is that both peoples influenced each other culturally, but not genetically. Unlike the seafaring Vikings, the Celts were more focused on cultivating their own lands than plundering neighboring lands. The Celts migrated to Ireland and Scotland, while the Germanic peoples settled mainly in Scandinavia. During the Viking Age, the Celts had a greater impact on the Vikings in terms of culture and language, as they had already been Christianized in the 5th century. The Vikings arrived in Ireland around the 7th century after conducting raids and pillaging in eastern England and Scotland. They played a significant role in founding some of Ireland's most famous cities, including Dublin and Cork. This indicates that there was not only violence but also diplomacy and trade between the two groups. The ancient Celtic tribes did not invent their own Runic language but adopted it because of Norse influence during a period of feuds and social interactions. These individuals were a mixture of Norse and Irish, known as Gaels. During the height of the Viking Age, around the 9th century, Viking settlers in Ireland and Scotland assimilated into the local populations, adopting their language and customs. This process, known as "Gaelicization," led to a significant transformation of their culture within a few generations. In fact, their culture can be seen more as Gaelic than Norse. Even after the conversion to Christianity and the disappearance of the Norse Gaels as a distinct group, they left a lasting impact on Ireland and Scotland. Many Irish towns still bear Norse-Gaelic names.

THE NORSE RELIGION

Similar to other complex religions, the Norse religion included two main components: rituals and esoteric knowledge that enabled individuals to understand the inner workings of the universe and discover their spiritual side. Regarding rituals and methods of deity worship, limited information is available. It is evident that the Norse gods had a devoted religious following that met the social, spiritual and psychological needs of the Vikings. However, myths and legends offer little information about the actual practices of divine worship. Historical sources mention the Norse Blót, a ceremony that celebrated Odin and other significant deities. Blót were typically held in temples or designated "blót houses" and involved sacrifices, both human and animal. To honor the deities, enemies were often sacrificed. Animals were used, when a specific deity had an animal with which he could be associated, such as Freyr with wild boars. The ceremony is vaguely reminiscent of modern Christian communion, where the animal was seen as the embodiment of the gods. Blót were a central aspect of Viking life, which led the month of November to be called "Blotmonth" or "Bloodmonth" in honor of divine ceremonies. Ancient Anglo-Saxon writings mention mass sacrifices of cattle and horses, with blood collected in special vessels for consumption or "sprinkled" on ceremony participants. Afterwards, a priest would bless the meat, vessels and chalices used during the banquet and festivities. Many times ceremonies were held to pay homage to specific deities. First, Odin, to bless the ruling class, followed by Freya and Freyr to bring peace and a prosperous harvest. Participants could also pour a chalice in honor of deceased loved ones. Viking sacrifices were seen as offerings to the gods in gratitude for their blessings and for maintaining order and harmony in the cosmos. The Norse did not perceive their deities as perfect or omnipotent; instead, they believed that the gods were subject to the fate and laws of the world. The Vikings regarded them primarily as guardians of order, restraining the forces of evil and rarely intervening in the events of the "mortal" world. Given the dangerous and harsh nature of the Viking world, it is not surprising that the Christian depiction of a loving and all-powerful God did not thrive in the minds and hearts of the Norse. They worshipped their gods with the hope that, in return, their families and community would be blessed and protected.

A significant part of the mystical knowledge possessed by the Vikings came from their myths and legends. These tales, which revolved around the realm of the gods and the creation of the cosmos, provided the Vikings with ideals, models and goals to incorporate into their lives. Odin, for example, served as a role model for kings, seekers of knowledge, and fathers, while Thor embodied the quintessential Viking characteristics of a warrior, loyalty, and determination to do one's duty to the end. In addition, figures such as Freya, Frigg and Freyr symbolized motherhood, the joy of life, Norse magic, wealth, peace and prosperity. The Vikings recognized the importance of all aspects represented by these deities in leading a happy life and building a successful society, as evidenced by the symbolic peace established between the Aesir and Vanir. The Norse tales also contained hidden elements and numerology that only sages and experts could unveil, enabling them to engage in divination and Seidr to foretell and influence destinies. It is evident that Viking spirituality was deep and more intricate than other peoples believed at the time. However, toward the end of the Viking era, the native population began to abandon their gods and traditions and embrace Christianity. Despite dramatic stories of forced conversions, the reality was that Christianity entered the Norse world naturally and gradually. The Vikings showed flexibility in their beliefs, incorporating Christian elements into their religion as soon as they encountered European lands. While some individuals clung to their own traditions, most Scandinavians were open to inclusion and chose to accept Christian elements incrementally rather than undergo complete conversion. As a result, Norse iconography merged with Christian symbols and customs to form a hybrid religion. It was considered acceptable for baptized Norse individuals to still seek Thor's protection in times of need. Conversion to Christianity among the Norse population was a gradual process that began before the involvement of Christian missionaries. The challenge for the clergy was not to teach the values and practices of Christianity, but rather to persuade others to embrace Christian elements exclusively by renouncing their pagan beliefs. The conversion to Christianity did not occur as an isolated event but rather coincided with the "Europeanization" of the Vikings, prompting them to abandon traditional values and beliefs. Moving from chieftains to kings, adopting the Latin alphabet and gradually conforming to European standards, the Vikings underwent a significant transformation.

However, the main reason for the transition to Christianity remains unclear. Although certainty eludes us, the most plausible explanation lies in the selfish inclinations of the Vikings. It is worth noting that their adherence to the deities was driven by the aspiration for protection, blessings and prosperity. However, the Norse gods had limitations. They showed ambivalence and lacked the ability to save the soul, often ignoring the appeals of mere mortals. In contrast, the Christian God embodied kindness, unwavering love and forgiveness. Consequently, the Vikings prioritized the entity that could provide the greatest benefits, making the adoption of Christianity an easy decision. The benefits it offered were considered substantial enough to warrant unlimited devotion and worship. In particular, Viking kings and rulers generally led the way in embracing Christianity because it facilitated the formation of influential alliances. Consequently, when a king converted, his subjects were likely to follow suit. Over time, Christianity gradually became the prevailing belief system, transforming the once pagan Vikings into devout adherents of the Christian faith.

02
THE ORIGIN OF THE WORLD

The world began with the element fire. From the initial state of chaos, devoid of any distinction between day and night, land and sea, life and death, a small spark emerged. This flame, fueled by an insatiable hunger, turned into a raging inferno called Muspelheim, a scorching, radiant realm that spewed rivers of fire and blasts of boiling air into the surrounding void. With the creation of heat and light, their opposites also came to light. On the other side of the universe, another world called Niflheim materialized, shrouded in icy darkness and deadly cold. A poisonous, icy wind gradually blew from Niflheim, resembling a slow river of enveloping ice. The collision of ice and fire in the void caused catastrophic explosions, filling the void with flying embers, shattered ice fragments, splashing water, and floating vapors. It was from this collision that the ice giant Ymir was born. Possessing the strength, coldness and lethality of Niflheim's breath, Ymir also contained the fiery spark of life within it. As the sparks danced around Ymir, sweat drops gave birth to new giants. However, Ymir and his progeny were not the only creations that emerged from the melting ice. A cow named

Audhumbla took shape in the interplay of fire and ice, providing milk for Ymir and his children. Audhumbla was also thirsty and quenched her thirst by licking the ice. Under the strokes of her tongue, something new began to emerge: first, what appeared to be a mane, followed by a head, and finally, a complete figure rose from the ice, observing its surroundings. This being was called Buri and was the first among the gods. Buri possessed strength and beauty and desired others of his kind. So he created a son named Borr, who fell in love with the giantess Bestla. Bestla gave birth to sons, of whom Odin was the eldest. Odin and his brothers waged a long and bloody war against Ymir. Although the war has been remembered for generations, its original causes were forgotten. It is likely that Ymir disapproved of his sons marrying gods, or perhaps both Odin and Ymir sought to claim dominion over the entire world. Regardless, they clashed, and in the end Odin and his brothers emerged victorious. Ymir succumbed, falling lifeless into the void that existed between the realms of fire and ice. His blood spread in a torrential flood, submerging the other frost giants except Bergelmir and his wife. In the midst of the chaos of the battle, Bergelmir built a magnificent ship, and during the deluge, he and his wife boarded it, sailing through the tide of blood to a safe place beyond the reach of the rising gods. Odin and his brothers devoted themselves to creation. They took Ymir's remains and fashioned them into a new world, positioned between the realms of ice and fire, blessed with running water and temperate air. Ymir's icy blood gave rise to lakes and seas, while his flesh and bones formed earth and mountains. His skull was positioned above this world, transforming into the arc of heaven. The gods retrieved fire from the sparks of Muspelheim and threw it into the air under the celestial dome to illuminate the world. At the outer edges of this world, beyond the boundless sea that surrounded it, was a wasteland inhabited by the descendants of Bergelmir. These giants, who carried with them the memory of Ymir's death, were waiting for an opportunity to take revenge. In the heart of the world, the gods erected a protective barrier made from Ymir's eyebrows, known as Midgard, to protect themselves from the giants. This fortified land became known as the realm of humans. After chaos and war, silence and order prevailed, marking the dawn of a new era. The sun gave warmth to the land, causing lush green plants to sprout and flourish. Odin and his brothers took two trees, fashioning them in the likeness of the gods and infusing them with life and inspiration. From these trees were born Ask and Embla, the first man and the first woman, giving birth to all the different peoples of the world. In addition, the gods transformed the worms that fed on Ymir's flesh into dwarves, endowing them with human form and wisdom. These dwarves coexisted with humans in the world, though not always harmoniously, as later stories will reveal.

THE BIRTH OF THE GODS

Ymir, known as "the Screamer," was the first living being born in Ginnungagap from the molten ice of Niflheim. Ymir was a hermaphrodite with the ability to reproduce independently, of immense size and endowed with great destructive power. During sleep, the sweat from his armpits gave birth to a man and a woman, while the sweat from his legs gave birth to another man, thus giving rise to the first frost giants. Also, from the persistent melting of the ice, there came into existence a creature called Audhumla, a cow. Audhumla, to feed herself, licked salty blocks of ice and generously provided rivers of milk for Ymir's nourishment and growth. While licking the ice, Audhumla unexpectedly discovered a man named Buri, the first of the Aesir gods. Buri, a rugged and attractive individual, had a son named Borr, who married Besla, the daughter of an ice giant. Borr and Bestla were the parents of Odin. Because of Borr's divine status and Bestla's giant heritage, Odin possessed a dual nature, being half god and half giant, making him a suitable leader for the Aesir tribe. This unlikely union of gods and giants gave birth to two more sons, Vili and Ve. Together with Odin, they shaped the rest of the world, comprising the sky, earth, vegetation, oceans and clouds.

THE CREATION OF HUMANS

One day, the sons of Borr, walking on the beach, found two logs, one of ash and one of elm. From the two pieces of wood they fashioned silhouettes, a man and a woman. Odin bestowed upon them the gift of life, Vili endowed them with physicality, speech, emotions and five senses, and Vé granted the ability to move, possess intellect and exercise their cognitive abilities. These humanoid creations were given the names Ask and Embla. Amazingly, it is from the lineage of these two individuals that the entire human race, whose home is Midgard, emerged. A man named Mundilfari soon met with the disfavor of the gods. He had two extraordinarily beautiful sons, one named Sol, who possessed kindness and grace, and the other named Mani, who exuded beauty and charm. The gods, perceiving this as an act of great presumption, chose to place these children in the heavens. Sol was given the responsibility of driving the horses Arvak and Alsvid, who pulled the chariot of the sun, a divine creation designed to illuminate the Earth. Similarly, Mani was tasked with guiding the moon on its celestial journey and governing its movements.

03
THE NORSE PANTHEON

The Norse people believed in gods and goddesses who were not only powerful and fearsome, but also wise and kind. These divine beings inspired many theories and stories about the creation of the world. Each god or goddess had their own personality traits and areas of influence and were seen as real beings who had a direct impact on people's lives. The term "pantheon" refers to the group of deities of a particular culture. The Norse pantheon included several groups of gods and goddesses, such as the Aesir, Vanir, and Jötnar, as well as minor deities and demigods. These divine beings were responsible for different aspects of the cosmos. However, the Norse Pantheon was vast and complex, making it difficult to list all the gods and goddesses. To understand it better, it helps to dwell on the most important ones worshipped during the Viking Age. The Norse Pantheon can be divided into three main groups: the Aesir (the new generation), the Vanir (the oldest), and the Jötnar (giants who were the first beings in the universe). After a long period of conflict, the Aesir emerged as the most powerful gods. The descriptions and powers of the deities vary depending on the source, with some features added or removed. This is especially evident when it comes to female deities, as their attributes are sometimes ascribed to male deities, reflecting a more patriarchal focus. Let us now try to provide some clarity.

THE AESIR

ODIN

Odin is a powerful and wise god in Norse mythology. He is the ruler of the Aesir gods and the king of Asgard. He has many different names such as Gangleri, Odinn, Othinn, Vak and Valtam. Odin is known as the Almighty and is responsible for war, death and knowledge. He is associated with many other things such as the gallows, healing, magic, poetry, kingship, shamanism, witchcraft, wisdom and the runic alphabet. He is credited with naming the day Wednesday (Woden Day). Odin's parents are Borr and Bestla. Borr is the son of Buri, the first Norse god, and Bestla is the daughter of the giant Bölthorn. Buri was created when the cow Audhumbla licked the salt ice of Ginnungagap to survive and feed Ymir, the first ice giant. Odin had several relationships, from which children were born. With the enchanting Frigg, he begat the noble Baldr, the enigmatic Hodr and the valiant Hermod. From the union with Jord was born the mighty Thor. In addition, the resolute Grid gave him the indomitable Vidar. However, the sagas woven by Snorri Sturluson reveal yet another aspect of Odin's authorship, attributing to him the birth of the esteemed

Bragi, the vigilant Heimdallr, the enigmatic Höd and the valiant Týr. However, alternative interpretations propose that these descendants, particularly the valiant Týr, owe their existence to another divine progenitor.

THOR

Thor is a character in Norse mythology known to be the god of thunder and lightning. Many people are familiar with the superhero Thor through the film sagas, but the Norse god is slightly different. He is the son of Odin and Jord, so Thor is also a giant, since his mother belongs to the Jottnar (Giant) race. He is greatly admired and revered, partly because he embodies the qualities of an ideal warrior. He is brave, strong and a loyal protector of Asgard. Along with a belt that gives him strength, Thor is most famous for his hammer, Mjöllnir, a term meaning "lightning." The Norse attributed thunderstorms to the hammer wielded by the thunder god. When the sound of thunder rang out and flashes of lightning lit up the sky, it was believed to be Thor crossing the skies in his chariot. According to mythology, Thor possessed the ability to influence rainfall and help crops grow lushly.

TYR

A Norse god known for his courage and justice, Tyr was a very important god in Norse mythology, but during the Viking period he became less popular. Before then, he was even considered the most powerful god. Tyr is also known by other names, such as Teiws, Tiw, T'waz, Cyo, Tius, Tio, and

Ziu. He is believed to be a continuation of Dyeus, who was the prototype of the Father God, in the ancient Proto-Indo-European period. Tyr was seen as the father of the gods before Odin became more important. Some versions of his story even say that he is Odin's son. Tyr was also known as the god of war in Norse mythology. However, when the Vikings came to power, Odin and Thor became more popular and Tyr's importance declined. It is thought that the Vikings did not appreciate Tyr's qualities, which focused on bravery and courage in battle.

GEFJUN

According to Norse legend, Gefjun entertained the Swedish king Gylfi, who promised him land as a reward. Gefjun then turned his four sons into oxen, and attached them to a plow. They dug up the land with such force that it was flooded by sea water, resulting in the formation of a lake. The excavated land was later dragged westward, eventually creating the island of Sjælland in Denmark. Some sources suggest that Gefjun performed this extraordinary task under the instructions of the deity Odin. She is the goddess of abundance and agriculture. Gefion's fountain in Copenhagen, Denmark, by Danish artist Anders Bundgaard, and dated 1908, depicts this story. Gefjun's (or Gefion's) name means "giver" or "generous," a peculiarity of the goddess. Most stories featuring Gefjun tell of her help to farmers.

BALDR

Son of Odin and Frigg, he was a highly respected god in Asgard. He was known to represent light, beauty and joy. Baldr, also called Balder or Baldur, was married to Nanna and together they had two children named Nep and Forseti. Baldr lived in a place called Breidablik. Of all the gods, Baldr was considered the most attractive, as he radiated his own light and had hair as white as snow.

SIF

Sif, a goddess of Norse mythology, was known as Thor's wife and the goddess of the harvest. In the Thor films, she is played by Jaimie Alexander, but unlike her character in the film, Sif actually had golden hair. Her hair became a source of trouble when Loki, in his mischievous ways, secretly cut it off. Sif was very upset and, as a result, the earth became barren and crops did not grow. This angered Thor, who confronted Loki and made him fix the situation. Loki convinced the dwarf brothers, known as the Sons of Ivaldi, a lineage of dwarf-artisans with the ability to create magical objects to create new golden hair for Sif.

BRAGI

He is the god of poetry and music and is known as the patron of poets. He is the son of Odin and Frigg and is married to Iðunn, who is the goddess of youth and apples. Bragi is often depicted as an old man with a long white beard, holding a golden harp and having runes engraved on his tongue. He used his music to welcome fallen warriors to Valhalla. According to one story, Bragi was a real person named Bragi Boddason who lived in the 9th century. He was a well-known and highly regarded poet in his time, and his fellow poets respected him so much that they added him to Norse mythology and made him a god.

IDUN

She is a goddess who bears special fruits that cause gods to stay young and live forever. A famous story about her involves her abduction by Loki. Loki was dealing with a giant pretending to be an eagle. Eventually, the eagle grabbed Loki and began to fly away with him. Loki wanted the eagle to let him go, but the eagle said he would only do so if Loki brought him the goddess called Idun. The eagle was actually aiming for the special fruit of immortality. Loki tricked Idun into leaving Asgard by telling her that there were better fruits outside the city walls. When she left the safety of Asgard, the eagle took her away.

VIDAR

The Great Ruler, he is also called Vidarr, Vithar and Vitharr. He is known as the god of vengeance and silence and was born of Odin and Grior. It has been foretold that he will avenge Odin's death during Ragnarok by stabbing Fenrir in the heart. Some stories also say that Vidar killed the wolf by stepping on his lower jaw and pulling his upper jaw until it broke. For this reason, Vidar is famous for wearing durable shoes made from pieces of leather donated over time by the people of Midgard. Vidar's revenge took place after the swollen sea and Surtr's fire subsided and allowed the "Silent God" to proceed with his intended task.

SIGYN

She is the bride of Loki. Although there are not many stories about her, there is one that shows her deep love for Loki. In this story, Loki convinced another god to unwittingly kill Baldur, which led the other gods to punish him. They imprisoned Loki in a cave and made him drip poison from a poisonous snake. To protect Loki from the poison, Sigyn sat beside him and held a bowl to collect the poison.

HÖD

The blind god, known as Hod, Hodr, Hoder and Hodur, had different names like the other gods. He was the son of Odin and Frigg and had a twin brother named Baldr who was loved by all. Hod was the god associated with winter and darkness. Unfortunately, Hod mistakenly killed Baldr after being tricked by Loki. As a result, Vali, who was born specifically to avenge Baldr, killed Hod.

FORSETI

Forseti, son of Baldr and Nanna, was a god known for his role in resolving conflicts and promoting peace. He was often called "the presiding one" because he listened to disputes and helped people find a way to reconcile. Forseti lived in a magnificent hall called Glitnir, which had a silver roof and golden pillars that shone brightly from afar. He was also associated with the practice of meditation.

FRIGG

Frigg is married to Odin and is the most important goddess of Asgard. She has special abilities called seidr, which allow her to see into the future and potentially alter it. Some Norse women who practiced seidr used it in exchange for basic necessities such as food and shelter. Frigg's name, "beloved," symbolizes her association with love and marriage.

VILI AND VE

The name Vili means "will" and is sometimes called the God of motivation. When Vili, Ve and Odin formed the first human beings, Vili gave them the power to think and feel emotions. The name Ve means "temple" and is considered the God of the divine, who oversees all things related to the gods. After Vili granted the first humans the ability to think and love, Ve granted them the ability to speak, see and hear.

LOKI

Loki is known to be the trickster god. While the other gods have strong relationships with each other, Loki is seen as an outcast. Loki's fame in Norse mythology also extended to members of his family. According to stories, Loki's parents are Jötunn Fárbauti and a woman named Laufey. Some scholars believe that Laufey may have been a member of the Aesir, which may explain why Loki is sometimes called "Laufeyjarson." His mother's lineage may have given him access to the halls where the gods and goddesses reside. On the other hand, Loki's connection to fire may have come from his father Fárbauti. Loki has two brothers named Helblindi and Býleistr. Although there is uncertainty about Loki's parents, there is clearer information about his wife and children. His wife, Sigyn, is also a member of the Aesir and remains loyal to Loki, regardless of his actions toward the rest of the gods. They have two sons, named Váli and Narfi. Loki can be mischievous and funny, but he is often described as a negative character. Many stories show Loki's tricks that lead to deception and trouble. One such story involves Loki cutting the golden hair of Thor's wife, Sif. This angers Thor and Loki promises to get new hair to avoid punishment. He seeks the help of the skilled dwarves of Nidavellir, who create new hair for Sif.

HEIMDALL

Another of Odin's children is Heimdall, born of nine different mothers, and known as the god of light and protection. He has the special ability to foresee the future and also has incredibly keen sight and hearing. He can see things that are hundreds of miles away, even in darkness. He calls himself Gullintani, a name derived from his golden teeth. Heimdall has a hall called Himinbjorg, where there was the beginning of Ragnarok. His main job is to protect the Bifrost, a bridge connecting several kingdoms, from any unwanted visitors, especially giants. His home is located at the top of the Bifrost, so he guards it at all times. He rarely sleeps and has a special horn called Gjallarhorn, which he uses to warn the gods of Asgard if there are intruders. She also has a horse named Gulltopp, which has a mane of gold. Heimdall eventually died during Ragnarok, but not before killing Loki.

THE VANIR

NJORD

Njord is a special god who belongs to two different groups of gods, the Vanir and the Aesir. He originally belonged to the Vanir group but had to go to live with the Aesir as a prisoner during a war between the two groups. Njord had the special task of controlling the wind and the sea, which made him very important for sailors who wanted to travel safely. He is associated with fertility and wealth. Njord had two children named Freyr and Freya, and some stories say their mother was a goddess named Nerthus. He married a giantess named Skadi, but they did not stay together long.

FREYA

She is known for her ability to control desires, and is considered a shamanic seer. Loki accused Freya of having relations with gods and elves, which may be why she was often associated with pleasure. Freya was also made an honorary member of the Aesir tribe, along with her father and brother. Freya has often been confused with Frigga, who is very similar to her. She was married to Odr, with whom she had two daughters named Hnoss and Gersemi. Freya was head of the Fólkvangr, and took care of warriors who died in battle. She lived in her dwelling called Sessrúmnir.

ULL

Ull was a god known for his role in ensuring justice. He was also recognized as a versatile god as well as an outstanding hunter. Ull had various names such as Oller, Uller, Ullr, Valder, and Vuldr. He was born to Sif, and his father was supposedly Egill-Örvandill, a famous archer who probably inspired Ull in life. He resided in Ydalir. While many consider Ull part of the Aesir tribe, some believe he came from the Vanir. Ull was described as a charming being with the characteristics of a skilled warrior. It is believed that Ull possessed magical abilities and used a special bone to travel, especially across the sea. Ull temporarily took Odin's place as ruler of Asgard when Odin was banished for ten years. Some sources suggest that Ull had connections with the elves of Völundarkviða.

ÓÐR

Óðr is a god in Norse mythology. He is part of the group called Vanir. He is married to a goddess named Freia and they have two children, Hnoss and Gersemi. We do not know much about Óðr, but we do know that he made long journeys and stayed away from home for a long time. Freia wept special tears made of gold because of his long absence. The name Óðr means "possessed" and is similar to the name of another important god called Odin. Like Odin, Óðr is connected to magic and long journeys. It is thought that Óðr may have been one of the many hostages given by the Aesir to the Vanir.

FREYR

He is part of the group called Vanir, but has a friendly relationship with the group Aesir. Freyr is loved by the Norse because he brings good things such as money, peace, health and abundance of harvest. Freyr lives in a place called Alfheim with some magical creatures called elves. When Loki helped bring back Thor's hammer, Freyr was given a special ship and a boar, Gullinbursti, as a gift.

NERTHUS

Nerthus is the sister of Njord and symbolizes Mother Earth. She is a goddess who values peace and those who worship her locked up their weapons when they thought she would visit their homes or community. Other than her love of nonviolence, nothing else is known about Nerthus.

JÖTNAR

The term Jötnar (Jötun in the singular), meaning giant, refers to those beings living under or among rocks. These entities, deeply intertwined with the natural world, have long been adversaries of the Æsir and Vanir since ancient times. Although they often assume the role of adversaries of the Aesir, some narratives depict them as victims of attacks by the gods, while others show them achieving triumphs over the deities. The Jötun (singular), dwell in the frigid realm of Jötunheim, which is closely connected to Midgard through mountain ranges and dense forests, while the fire giants inhabit Múspellsheimr, the realm of fire. They play a key role in the dramatic finale of Ragnarök, in which the tree Yggdrasil is given to the flames. Various types of giants are present in the tales: clay giants, fire giants, mountain giants, sea giants, wind giants, and frost giants. Sometimes these giants display characteristics associated with their habitats; for example, Surtr possesses the power to generate or control fire. Others, such as Aegir and his wife Rán, reside on an island in a hall near the waves, earning them the nickname sea giants. These beings symbolize the primordial forces of chaos and destruction, juxtaposed with the divine figure representing life and order.

AEGIR AND RAN

Aegir, the deity associated with the ocean, possesses dominion over all sea creatures. He is married to Ran, the goddess who symbolizes the sea and serves as the progenitor of the nine maidens of the waves, considered the spirits of the waves. Aegir and Ran both belong to the Jotunn lineage, a race of giants long at odds with the Aesir gods. However, they maintain friendly relations with the Asgardian deities, often receiving invitations to attend their banquets. Aegir is renowned for his hospitality, while Ran is known for his malevolent deeds, such as capsizing ships and drowning sailors, subsequently forcing them to dwell in his sunken realm.

HEL

Hel, a deity associated with death and the underworld, is depicted as a giantess in Norse mythology. She presides over Helheim, also known as Hel, a realm in which people who die of illness or old age are said to reside. Hel is believed to have originated from the union between Loki, a mischievous deity, and Angrboda, a giantess. According to Snorri's interpretation, Hel has two brothers, Fenrir, a wolf, and Jormungand, a serpent. However, some scholars question the accuracy of this account and claim that Hel may have been a creation of earlier scholars and poets. Similar to their father Loki, it is prophesied that these three brothers will bring trouble and tragedy.

MYTHICAL CREATURES

TROLLS

In some Swedish folklore, trolls are depicted as multi-headed monstrous entities that inhabit forests, mountains, or caves. The initial category of trolls, residing in mountains, is characterized by immense size, aggressive nature, limited intellect and slowness. Cave-dwelling trolls possess a shy nature, are shorter than humans, have stocky limbs, but are remarkably intelligent. These creatures exploit the environment to exert their power, safeguard themselves or remain hidden. The origin of these mythical beings can be traced back to the concept of giants (jötun) in their cosmology and kingdoms, as the Old Norse term for troll is jätte.

DWARVES

It is hard to imagine Thor without his reliable hammer Mjölnir, or Odin without his spear Gungnir. Similarly, Freyja's beauty is enhanced by the wonderful jewel Brísingamen. What do these objects have in common? They were all made by a group of skilled blacksmiths and craftsmen known as dwarves. Different groups or families of dwarves are responsible for creating various legendary things, ranging from the indestructible ribbon called Gleipnir, to the objects of the deity Freyr, such as his boar and his ship. The Poetic Edda and the Prose Edda give slightly different explanations of the origin of the dwarves. While both books mention that they came from Ymir's body, the former suggests that they were spontaneously generated from the giant's blood and bones. On the other hand, the latter states that the dwarves were mindless parasites who became part of the giant's flesh, but later received intelligence from the gods. Both books provide a list of various dwarves, some of whom are better known than others. Four dwarves in particular, named Norðri, Suðri, Austri and Vestri, have the specific task of holding up the sky.

NORNS

The Norns are not exactly goddesses, giants or dwarves, but neither are they exactly human. They are primarily female beings who have the important role of predicting and controlling the fates of all living beings, including the Aesir and others. The Norns are not limited only to Urd, Verdandi and Skuld; there are many others who are said to appear when a child is born and predict the child's future. For this reason, some Norns are seen as kind and helpful, while others are seen as harmful and malignant.

DÍSIR

Disir are female spirits who have control over the lives of people and their families. The main difference is that they come from a combination of the spirits of family ancestors. These spirits act as protectors, taking care of the future of their descendants. To show respect for these spirits, people held festivals where they made sacrifices and said prayers in hopes of gaining their support.

HUMANS

According to the Poetic Edda, the first man was named "Ask" and the first woman was named Embla. They were named after different kinds of trees: "Ask" from the ash tree and "Embla" from the elm or vine. Stories about how they were created differ, with some saying Odin, Hönir and Lothur gave them special gifts, while others say Odin and his brothers Vili and Vé were involved.

ELVES

According to references in popular culture, elves are renowned for their beauty, tall stature, skill in battle, and mastery of magic. Originally, in pre-Christian mythology, these semi-divine beings constituted a distinctive group that dwelt in a single realm. Over time, their mythology evolved, resulting in their classification into two factions: the Light Elves (Ljósáfar), who resided in the realm of Alfheim under the rule of the deity Freyr, and the Dark Elves (Dökkálfar), who dwelt in the depths of the earth and possessed a darker complexion. Elves were believed to inflict disease on humans, but could also provide cures when offered something in return. In addition, there was a correlation between elf worship and ancestor veneration, as humans were said to turn into elves after their death.

04
NORSE RELIGIOUS PRACTICES

In the past, people who followed the pagan Germanic religion often performed their rituals near bodies of water such as lakes and swamps. They believed that these places were sacred and allowed them to connect with the divine. This is why archaeologists found many wooden figures depicting people with emphasized sexual traits in these areas, suggesting that they were offerings to fertility deities. Sacrifices were an important part of Norse/Germanic religion, and the ancients believed that making sacrifices in a place inaccessible to humans would ensure that the gods would be reached. They often burned or threw sacrificial objects into lakes, accompanied by feasts with lots of food and drink. They also used carved wooden figures or even people to sacrifice by weighing them down with stones and throwing them into swamps. These victims were usually believed to be witches who brought bad luck to the community. Bogs were a favorite place for sacrifices because, according to beliefs, the bodies did not dissolve and were preserved in an intermediate state between the human world and the afterlife. The Norse also sometimes offered their weapons to the gods, usually those taken from enemies they had killed or conquered. Norse paganism is very different from Christianity and other religions in that it has unique methods of celebrating feasts and festivals. These celebrations are not led by priests but instead focus on honoring and worshiping deities, whose figures change from one geographical area to another. However, all these belief systems have one thing in common: they are linked to important events and have significant value for the entire community, not just individuals. Each holiday is carried out with a specific ritual performed by the one who has a superior role in the community. In ancient times, these individuals held positions of power such as kings or leaders within the villages. Currently, this responsibility falls to the head of the household or spiritual leader of the Asatru community. The ceremonies often involve a sacrificial offering, known as a blot among the Asatruar. Typically, this sacrifice involves slaughtering an animal, extracting its blood and presenting it to the gods. Afterwards, the meat is boiled and shared among members of the community. This pagan method of worshipping the gods is observed today mainly on a local scale. However, in ancient times, blot ceremonies were widespread and celebrated throughout Scandinavia. Daily rituals are a common part of the pagan way of life. These can be fulfilled through a small sacrifice or the implementation of a simple incantation. They are performed with the intention of achieving prosperity, longevity, fertility, a safe journey or anything else deemed significant to the individual or community. These benefits could be granted to all, provided they were pleasing to the gods, who were the ultimate providers of all desired outcomes. In addition to these daily rituals, there are some other noteworthy ceremonies that were and still are an integral part of the practice of Norse paganism. One such example is the ritual performed at the birth and naming of a child, during which devotees offer prayers to the Norse goddesses Freya and Frigg. Initially, galdr songs are sung to implore the goddesses for a safe and successful birthing experience. If the baby is born and survives the nine nights, it is placed in the father's lap and sprinkled with water. Throughout this process, the child is given a name and welcomed into the family with the blessing of the gods. According to the Asatruar, this occasion not only brings joy to the family but also symbolizes the expansion of the entire society. Wedding ceremonies also have great significance within Norse paganism, as they mark the beginning of family life and all the positive aspects associated with it. After the wedding ceremony, a series of smaller rituals are generally performed. These culminate in an elegant wedding banquet and ceremony. This ritual will be performed for the next 50 years of the family's existence. Similar to other holidays, wedding rituals are conducted to ask the gods' blessings on the betrothed couple and their union. This was especially crucial in ancient times, when marriage represented the legal union of two families. Although circumstances have changed in modern times, marriage remains a spiritually binding contract for the

Asatruar. Finally, another ceremony highly valued by Norse pagans is the burial of loved ones and the performance of funeral rites. Followers of Norse paganism attach great importance to the lives of individuals on earth and the rewards that can be obtained during their lives. However, this does not imply a disdain for the afterlife. Similar to other religions, their funeral rites consist of cremation or burial ceremonies. In the past, cremation was the most popular method of sending someone on their final journey. In addition to cremation, it included literal burial of the remains along with a means of transportation. Whether it was a horse, wagon, or even a small boat, the purpose was to ensure that the deceased arrived safely at their final destination. Unfortunately, there is limited information available on burial and cremation rituals.

NORSE FESTIVALS

In ancient Norse times there were only two seasons each year: summer and winter. Summer began around the spring equinox and was celebrated with a festival called Ostara. Winter began after the autumnal equinox and was characterized by celebrations of winter nights. These two festivals were very important and are celebrated by all Asatru communities even today. Along with these were many other festivals, some larger like Yule and some less significant. Some of these festivals still involve small sacrifices, while others have evolved into gatherings with family and friends. Despite changes in the ways they are celebrated, the traditions have remained the same, and some of them are still named Blot, in reference to the sacrifices that were once made. Although most of these festivals are still present in modern paganism, not all of them are included in the practices of modern Asatru. In keeping with the principles of Norse paganism, these actions were and continue to be undertaken with due consideration for the welfare of the entire community and, above all, its individual members.

YULE

Yule, which begins on December 20, is a well-known Nordic holiday for several reasons. First, it represents the darkest time of the year when daylight hours are shortest. The beginning of Yule signifies a new beginning and the optimistic anticipation of a more favorable year to come. According to ancient Norse legends, Yule heralds the return of the deity Baldur from the realm of Hel, thus beginning the gradual loosening of the grip of winter on Earth and the beginning of the less cold season. For a duration of twelve nights, Yule is commemorated through numerous festivals, characterized by feasts, melodious performances and the exchange of gifts. The festival's appellation comes from the Norwegian word "HJOL," meaning wheel, which represents the lowest point in the cycle of the year preparing for rejuvenation. The initial evening of Yule, known as Mother's Night, traditionally begins with homage to the goddess Frigga and the veneration of the ancestral female spirits known as Disir, in order to honor and recognize all women during this period of rebirth. To ensure the occurrence of this rebirth and the subsequent rising of the Sun, a customary vigil is observed on this night. Subsequent days and nights are devoted to celebrating the new beginning by engaging in communal gatherings, sharing melodic performances and indulging in culinary delights, even extending the invitation, figuratively speaking, to the dead. Norse pagans often use various baked goods and ornaments, such as the sun wheel or Yule tree, to offer a warm welcome to all who enter their lives.

MABON

Mabon or Haustblot, being a minor holiday, has fewer documented instances of feasting than other holidays. It usually takes place around September 22 and marks the culmination of the harvest season. In the past, individuals, particularly those in farming communities, were busy harvesting, leaving them insufficient time to organize elaborate feasts as they would have done for other holidays. However, small-scale sacred ritual celebrations were conducted as tribute to the harvest deities, namely Frey, Nerthus, Iduna and Njord. Gratitude was expressed toward Jord for his contribution, along with Snotra, the goddess associated with labor and hospitality. Huldra, who oversees animal care, is honored for facilitating the raising of livestock during the colder months. For followers of Asatruar, this festival remains an occasion of solemnity, marked by the lighting of bonfires, banquets and dances of the autumnal equinox. Gathering around these fires, which serve as the sole source of illumination, families and entire pagan communities often unite and strengthen their bonds by sharing ancient tales. This tradition was originally practiced to avoid the dangers of solitude and vulnerability to the dangers of the coming season. As the second harvest festival of the year, Mabon is also an opportunity to express gratitude and commemorate the successful completion of another season of arduous labor. Through collective participation, people are able to take part in all these activities and foster a stronger sense of community.

WINTER NIGHTS

Although they symbolize the beginning of the harsh winter season, winter nights are often marked by a deep ceremonial tradition. Ancestors are revered and their assistance or guidance is awaited for the coming year. This festival, which runs from October 29 to November 1, is believed to have the power to foretell the fate of many individuals. Animals that would not survive the winter were often sacrificed for this purpose. It is customary to engage in personal sacrifice for the betterment of the community and to repel evil spirits. Unlike many other rituals, this task is often assumed by the matriarch of a family, as she is considered the ultimate protector of the home and family. As a result, safeguarding the home becomes much more likely. On this occasion, Hela, the deity of the dead, and Mordgud, the guardian of the Underworld, are worshipped as the new rulers of the ancestors. Nidhogg, the dragon who devours corpses, is implored to spare them, while Hlin, the goddess of sorrow, and Hermod, the messenger of the gods who travels the road to Hel, are invoked to provide comfort to both the living and the dead. Another prevalent way of observing this festival involves sanctification and leaving the last sheaf in the field for Odin to discover. Later he can take it with him during the Wild Hunt, when he will face spectres and other ethereal entities after the winter nights. By leaving the fields to Odin, individuals can engage in introspection and contemplate their actions of the previous year, thus striving to improve their conduct in the next.

MIDSUMMER

The summer solstice, a holiday celebrating the longest day of the year, falls on June 21 in the northern hemisphere. Although it is a time of joy and elation, it also has a somber undertone. After this occasion, the days begin to get shorter and darker. They signal the approach of winter, and this prompts reflection and introspection. It is believed that the god of light, Baldur, died during this time, initially causing great despair among the Aesir. However, they eventually overcame the moment and moved on, learning a timeless lesson on how to face life's challenges and move forward. Midsummer provides an opportunity to offer blessings and engage in practices that honor the sun, receiving its life-giving light and gifts in return. In addition, Dagr, the god of the day, is also worshipped during this period. Traditionally, the evening of the summer solstice includes bonfires, speeches, traditional songs and dances.

THORRABLOT

This is a festival deeply rooted in Viking traditions that continues to be celebrated by a portion of the Icelandic population. Although it is recognized as a cultural celebration, for pagans this holiday has special significance as it is an occasion to honor Thor or the winter deity Thorri, or sometimes both. Originally, this festival involved sacrificial offerings to the gods. However, with the Christianization of Iceland, it was abolished, only to be revived in the 19th century. During Thorrablot, after a large banquet, group activities, singing, storytelling and drinking follow. Afterwards, the festivities turn to dancing, which often continues until the early morning hours, when the festivities come to an end. This occasion serves as an opportunity to express gratitude to the gods for the abundant gifts and blessings bestowed on humanity.

DISTING

During this festival, tribute is paid to the deities associated with fertility and the rebirth of spring. This day indicates the arrival of a new season, signaling the gradual cessation of winter's rigors. It is commonly called "Plow Enchantment," during which the plow and other agricultural implements are sanctified and offerings are presented to the gods in pursuit of a fruitful season. After the plow is blessed, a ceremonial furrow is dug and filled with sweets and other gifts. Numerous individuals participate in the festivities, expressing their reverence and gratitude to the gods who bestow blessings and help upon them. The Disting festival takes place during the winter season, allowing the darker aspects of the festival to be celebrated. In addition, the deity Odin, is commemorated and worshipped during this time. It serves as a time of confidence and optimism for the approaching spring, which coincides with the rebirth of many activities. It is an opportunity to express gratitude to the earth, which nourishes and sustains us even in the darkest of times. Although modern society no longer relies on the land and agricultural tools for sustenance, many still commemorate this holiday because it provides an opportunity to establish a deeper connection with the land itself. To best represent this occasion, numerous individuals engage in the act of planting seeds or trees and presenting offerings to the gods.

OSTARA

Ostara is a festival held annually on March 21, and coincides with the spring equinox. It marks the beginning of the summer months and is named after Ostara, a Germanic goddess who represents spring and the renewal of life. The festival celebrates Earth's return to life after a long, cold winter. According to tradition, residences are adorned with colored eggs, branches, etc. The hare was revered as the embodiment of the goddess Ostara, serving as her spiritual animal or sacred creature. The consumption of hare meat was sanctioned only with the approval of the goddess. The observance and preservation of the Ostara festival amplifies the memory of these ancient traditions.

WALPURSIG NIGHT OR MAY EVE

This occasion is celebrated on different days, from April 30 to May 1, depending on the country. In Germany, Finland and Sweden, May Eve is celebrated on April 30. This holiday is named after a lady called Valborg, Walpurgis, Valderburger or Wealdburg. Born in 710 in Britain, she was the niece of St. Boniface. Together with her brother, Wunibald, she went to Wurttemberg, Germany, where Wunibald founded the convent of Heidenheim. His sister, Walpurgis, became a nun in this convent. She died in 779 and was consecrated a saint on May 1 of the same year. Viking fertility festivals were celebrated on April 30, and since Walpurgis was declared a saint at the same time, her name was linked to Norse fertility celebrations. Walpurgis was worshipped, in a similar way in which the Vikings celebrated spring. This holiday is a major national holiday in Finland and Sweden, along with Midsummer and Yuletide. Pagans believe Freya is the ruler of this holiday because Walpurgis is the Germanic equivalent of Valentine's Day and Freya is the goddess of love and witchcraft. In Scandinavia, the May tree is carried in procession during this celebration, a tradition that dates back to the ancient pagan fertility procession. At night, fires are lit in high places and people jump on the flames for good luck and auspiciousness.

FREYFEST OR LAMMAS OR LITHASBLOT (JULY 31 ST.-AUG. 1 ST.)

Lammas is commonly believed to derive from the Anglicized term "hlaf-mass" or "feast of loaves," signifying a pre-Christian occasion to express gratitude for bread. Pagans commemorate this festival by producing bread in the likeness of Freyr, followed by a symbolic act of sacrifice and consumption. The arrival of the first fruits of the harvest, typically on August 1, prompts Germanic traditions to present the first bundle as an offering to pagan deities in appreciation. Within contemporary pagan practices, Lammas, also known as Lithasblot or Freyfest, is devoted to honor Freyr, the deity associated with fertility. So is Sif, the bride of Thor, whose flowing golden hair is believed to symbolize the abundant fields of ripe crops. In addition, Lammas represents a significant time for warriors, who return after the planting season with triumphant news from battle. Freyfest marks the beginning of arduous efforts in harvesting and preparing for the impending harsh winter months.

RITUALS AND SPELLS

In the past there was no structured religion, but spiritual practices closely related to magic were followed. Symbols were of great importance to society as a whole, but each community and family also had its own personal interpretations. Although magical healers were respected, they were not supported by any formal organization. Thus, when Christianity arrived, it was not unusual for the old Northern magic to be practiced along with the new religion. The old magic-based faith was known as "Forn Sidr" and Christianity was called "Nyr Sidr." Both involved sacred acts, rituals and worship of higher powers and, for the Norse, were not so different from each other. Norse magic and culture were often borrowed and modified as they spread among the Germanic tribes. Ideas about the meaning of magical rituals were passed down over time and across vast areas of the land, transforming traditions, spells, stories, and myths. Norse magic was influenced by this mix of different cultures but also had strong ties to the land and its people. For this reason, some celebrations were personalized. Sacrifices, feasts, and celebrations involving alcoholic beverages and food from animals sacrificed to the gods were common. These events were often held during specific seasons and aimed at improving fertility, ensuring success in battle or obtaining a good harvest. They were also used to ensure happy births, strong marriages, peaceful burials and a smooth transition to the afterlife. These rituals were often adapted to specific communities or individuals. However, the understanding of these practices is influenced by the spread of Christianity, which regarded Norse rituals as superstitious or related to demon worship. However, archaeological evidence, including the runic alphabet, has shed light on these ancient rituals. Some aspects may prove to be false, while others are easily recognized and understood. Both private and public rituals are likely to have taken place, with similarities between them. Let us now explore the most common and interesting rituals.

RITES OF PASSAGE

Linked to birth, death, and marriage, these rituals were commonly performed in both public and private settings. Childbirth was considered risky for both mother and child, so a ceremony involving Galdr chanting was often performed to ensure a safe delivery. Prayers were dedicated to the goddesses Freyja and Frigg. Nine nights after birth, a ceremony similar to Christian baptism was held, during which guests brought gifts and wished the baby well. Water was sprinkled on the baby while he/she was held by his/her father, symbolizing formal acceptance into the family. During this time, the baby was given a name, often in honor of ancestors or deities. The ceremony of being held in the father's lap marked the child's entry into society and made the parents responsible for his/her well-being.

MARRIAGE

In addition to the choice of spouse and the need for family approval, which was often decided primarily by other relatives, there were numerous rules and ceremonies designed to invoke divine blessings for the union and to prevent unfortunate marriages. However, it should be noted that these rituals did not guarantee immunity from marriage or separation, then as now. Engagement dates were carefully determined, while matters of inheritance, property and dowry were subject to negotiation. Once these matters were resolved, the divine approval of the gods was sought. The central ceremony was the wedding itself, known as brudlaup. This public event brought together the two families involved and included a banquet that lasted as long as three days. The goddess Var would attend the wedding vows. Freyja and Thor were invoked to bless the marriage with fertility and good fortune. Guests would accompany the bride and groom to the marital home, and witnesses would attest to the consummation of the marriage between the couple.

THE RITE OF BIRTH

Norse tradition attaches great importance to the conception and birth of a child. According to this belief system, it is believed that the spirit of the future child is created at conception. However, the spirit does not enter the child's body immediately, but enters gradually as the child grows and develops reason and intelligence. Before the spirit can fully incarnate, both the father and mother must acknowledge that the child's spirit existed prior to birth in Midgard. The actual birth of a child is considered a sacred event that serves as a connection between the physical and spiritual realms. To commemorate this significant occasion, a birth ritual is performed. This ritual serves as the child's first initiation and is intended to foster spiritual growth. During the ritual, the godhi or gydhja, a religious leader, recites ceremonial words while applying oil to the child's forehead. The ritual concludes by making the "sign of the hammer" and uttering additional words, although specific words and gestures may vary among practitioners and groups.

THE RITE OF DEATH

Many cultures and religions embrace the concept of an afterlife, in which the soul is believed to reside after the death of the physical body. It is commonly believed that heaven awaits those who have lived virtuous and righteous lives, while hell serves as a destination for those who have led dishonorable existences. Theories regarding the post-mortem experience vary according to individuals and religious beliefs. However, it remains uncertain what really happens after death. According to Norse mythology, there are two potential destinations for the deceased. The first, known as Valhalla, represents a highly esteemed abode where noble warriors who met their death valiantly in battle are granted the privilege of dining with the gods. On the other hand, those who have died due to illness, old age, natural causes or accidents are destined to Hel, which should not be misunderstood with the conventional concept of a place of torment. Instead, Hel serves as an alternative realm of the afterlife, providing comfort and reunion with loved ones. Contrary to what is seen in the movies, funeral rites do not involve the use of flaming boats where the deceased were burned. In the past, high-ranking individuals were buried inside mounds, containing items deemed necessary for the afterlife. Alternatively, funeral pyres were employed, as the massive columns of smoke were believed to assist in the spirit's ascension into the afterlife. Given the logistical challenges faced in contemporary times, such as the impracticality of erecting funeral pyres, modifications were introduced. Modern funeral rituals include the burial of the deceased accompanied by a replica of Thor's hammer or the placement of this artifact on the coffin lid. In the case of cremation, the replica of Thor's hammer is consigned to the flames along with the deceased.

ANCESTOR WORSHIP

Another custom practiced in Norse society was ancestor veneration, a ritual considered highly significant because it was believed that deceased ancestors retained the ability to influence the lives of their descendants. According to Norse cosmology, ancestors resided in an afterlife, the nature of which varied depending on the circumstances of their death. By conducting appropriate rituals and treating ancestors with the due reverence they deserved, the living could receive blessings and secure their own prosperity and happiness. Conversely, neglecting these rituals could result in curses, misfortune and even the summoning of malevolent elves. An integral aspect of ancestor worship involved the placement of sacred objects inside mounds located near family dwellings to safeguard the home and its inhabitants. In addition, this placement served the practical purpose of preventing grave raids.

WIGHTS WORSHIP

Earth wights were believed to be spiritual entities responsible for safeguarding the earth. Consequently, they were held in high regard and certain rules had to be followed to avoid conflict with them. Called "landvættir" in Old Norse, these spirits were believed to possess authority and influence over the earth and its inhabitants. They had the ability to bestow blessings or curses on individuals. Typically, women were given the task of caring for these earth spirits, offering them food and drink near areas such as forests and water sources where they were believed to reside. The use of runes, a key element in Norse rituals, served various purposes including communicating with deities and ancestors, divination, interpreting omens and invoking blessings or curses. Runes played a significant role in rituals, both used for drawing lots and as symbolic representations. Details of specific rituals and events remain uncertain, but information can be gathered from more recent historical sources, mainly from the sagas of the Scandinavian peoples. In one saga, Odin required sacrifices for a prosperous year in early winter, rebirth in midwinter, and a good harvest in summer. The dead were cremated and their ashes scattered in the sea or buried in the ground. The existence of graves and mounds further corroborates the sagas, validating their accounts. By combining archaeological evidence with written sources, we can form a general understanding of the rituals practiced in Norse magic, both in private and public settings. Place names, symbols, and runes associated with specific locations also provide insights into these rituals. For example, some places are translated as "Temple of Thor" in contemporary Scandinavian languages. Areas consecrated through rituals were called "ve," signifying the existence of special rules for that place. Burial sites were also designated for specific purposes. Jewelry and carved stones depicted images, symbols or runic letters that identified particular areas used for seid or other forms of magic, dating back to the Iron Age. These runes or symbols also indicated the titles or names of magical practitioners and their specific positions. These names suggest that rune masters practiced their art in specific locations and their work was recognized and marked as such. Written documents indicate the presence of specialists in different types of magic, affirming their status in Norse society. Those who practiced seidr and galdr were both revered and feared, often finding themselves isolated despite holding esteemed positions in society. Many individuals in positions of authority within Norse societies, whether in villages, as heads of households, or as rulers or kings, were also responsible for participating in ritual practices. These rituals were intended to ensure prosperity, success in battle, and resolution of problems related to everyday issues. Leaders who refused to take part in these practices, particularly as Christianity gained influence, often faced a loss of followers or were unable to preside over important seasonal occasions, including rituals and public events. During the transitional period when Christian and magical symbols coexisted, local rulers and leaders had to juggle a delicate balance between preserving ancient traditions and acknowledging the rise of the new faith.

SPELLS

In Norse magic, each spell had a symbol called a pentagram, which identified the arrangement of runes used to cast that spell. Runes were often engraved on rock or wood and were seen as an important alphabet and an essential part of spells. The spells showed that the runes themselves were fundamental and powerful in magic. Spells, along with rituals, were a crucial part of the practice of magic and it was essential that practitioners knew them accurately. If a spell was misinterpreted, it could result in a curse instead of a blessing, the loss of an important battle or a bad harvest. Although the Christian Church prohibited spells, they remained important even after the arrival of Christianity. In fact, their use became even more important after the Reformation, when Protestant practices became less ritualistic than those of the Catholic Church. Despite the strict ban imposed by the Lutheran Church in Scandinavia, the symbols became more widespread between 1664 and 1690, what became known as the new magical era. Runic invocations to create spells were common, both during the period when the Elder Futhark alphabet was created and centuries later. However, the specific uses of these spells have been lost because there are not enough historical records.

NORSE RELIGION IN MODERN PRACTICES

If you believe that Norse religion has completely disappeared, you will be surprised to learn that it still exists today. There are various groups of people around the world who actively participate in this religion, with a greater concentration in Europe and Scandinavia. They practice a modern version of the ancient pagan religion and call it paganism. However, the term "pagans," used to describe those who practice paganism, has historically been derogatory and is still viewed negatively in certain contexts. It originally referred to societies considered uncivilized for not converting to Christianity. Currently, paganism is seen as a new religious movement that seeks to reconstruct the ancient belief systems of the Norse/Germanic tribes and adapt them to the modern era. Practitioners of paganism strive to revive these ancient beliefs using whatever surviving historical evidence they can find. Similar to the ancient Norse religion, paganism is polytheistic and worships a pantheon of gods and goddesses, the same ones worshipped by the early Germanic tribes. Unlike Christianity, the gods and goddesses in pagan religion are not seen as perfect, omnipotent, or ever-present. They are believed to possess both strengths and weaknesses, and it is believed that they will eventually die, as depicted in Norse mythology with the death of Baldr.

05
MODERN NORSE RELIGION

ASATRU

Asatru, a modern Icelandic term, refers specifically to the worship and veneration of the Aesir gods. It is commonly used in formal contexts within the Asatru community, more so than the term "Norse paganism." Although Asatru followers recognize and believe in the Vanir gods, they do not speak of or worship any deities other than those of the Aesir tribe. Some attribute the emergence of Vanatru to the Asatruars' lack of involvement and commitment to the Vanir deities. Asatru is a polytheistic faith, with some deities such as Thor gaining more prominence in popular culture. However, over several centuries, Asatru was systematically dismantled and its non-Christian practices repressed. The dominant Christian Church demonized the pagan practices, eventually leading to Asatru's decline. However, its teachings and ideas survived through oral stories, traditions and folklore. The faith has experienced a revival in contemporary times through the Neopagan movement in Europe. Asatru follows a strict and conventional set of rules, which can foster a large formal community of adherents. In contrast, Northern Paganism emphasizes small-scale self-sufficient communities that uphold their own traditions, cultures, and belief systems. Although Heathenism and Asatru have roots in Northern Paganism, many modern Asatruars prefer to use the term Asatru because words such as Northern Paganism and Heathenism tend to have negative connotations for the general public. In particular, Asatru does not engage in missionary or proselytizing efforts, allowing people to join the community voluntarily and without obligation. Becoming a pagan involves no reward; it is solely a personal calling. Asatru is a faith guided primarily by instinct, in which practitioners worship and interact with gods in the way they see fit for them. Freedom of practice is one of the distinguishing characteristics that make Asatru attractive to its followers. Asatru priests have a pantheistic perspective and officiate at naming ceremonies, weddings, funerals, coming-of-age celebrations and other rituals. The Asatru Association, a formal Icelandic religious organization of paganism, was founded on the first day of summer in 1972 by Sveinbjörn Beinteinsson, a farmer and poet. This day, which falls on the first Thursday after April 18, is a national holiday in Iceland. The Asatru Association gained legal recognition and registration as a religious organization in 1973. The highest religious office within the association is that of "Allsherjargodi," an elective office. Each of Asatru's priests, known as godi, is assigned a congregation called a godord to lead. Although these godords are generally tied to specific geographical regions, individuals are not obliged to join any particular congregation and are free to choose one that suits their preferences. Legal recognition has enabled the organization to perform legally binding rituals and ceremonies, as well as to collect a portion of the church tax, which is levied on religious congregations to manage and support the churches and their staff. Sveinbjörn Beinteinsson was the organization's leader from its inception in 1972 until his death in 1993. During his tenure, membership remained below 100 and activity was limited. Asatru does not adhere to a fixed religion, theology or dogma, as each individual is free to hold his or her own beliefs. For example, many Wiccan members are also members of the Asatru Association. Asatru priests believe in a pantheistic perspective, and perform ceremonies such as weddings, funerals, coming-of-age celebrations and other rituals.

CORE TEACHINGS OF MODERN ASATRU PRACTICES

When embarking on a journey to embrace Northern Paganism, it is essential to prioritize active communication and engagement with the gods. In Pagan beliefs, gods are seen as companions, and conversing with them fosters a stronger relationship and facilitates understanding of one's path. Cultivating the habit of talking with the gods from the beginning is crucial, as modern life often distracts us from such spiritual interactions. However, with dedication, this practice can become as routine as maintaining a healthy lifestyle or engaging in exercise. It is important to recognize that deities manifest in various forms, such as spirits, and one can have conversations freely with each of them. There is no need to fear this interaction. Whether one is conversing with Odin, Thor or any other deity, it is essential to approach them with the utmost respect. Initially, during a conversation, it is not possible to fully understand the expectations of each god, but respect serves as a safe starting point. For example, when seeking an audience with Odin, the leader of the Norse pantheon, it is prudent to regard him as an esteemed father figure or guide who imparts wisdom and clarity of thought. In approaching Odin, one should use humility and respect, seeking his guidance and wisdom. In contrast, a different approach is warranted when interacting with a deity such as Loki. Although respect remains a vital component of any conversation, a more informal approach can be taken, treating Loki as a friend or ally. Loki is a deity who grants wishes but also expects something in return, thus establishing a sense of camaraderie rooted in reciprocity. Another significant aspect of conversing with Norse deities is having a purpose. What specific questions or concerns do you wish to address with your god? Do you seek enlightenment, clarity or solutions to problems? Casual conversations, such as discussing daily work experiences, should be avoided as they have no meaningful purpose and waste the gods' valuable time. It is critical to value the time spent with gods by ensuring that these interactions are meaningful. The second step in the Asatru journey involves gaining knowledge and wisdom. Thorough research is required to understand the foundations and complexities of the Asatru faith. This involves delving into its meaning, historical origins, the identities of the gods and goddesses, their distinguishing characteristics from humans, and the roles they play within Asatru. Acquiring information about Asatru's ancestors is also crucial.

As we delve into the history of our Viking and Germanic predecessors, we shed light on misconceptions that may have been incorporated into the narrative of Norse culture, either intentionally or inadvertently. It is essential to recognize the advanced intellect, courage, and nautical skill of our ancestors, who crossed great distances, conquered new lands, and assimilated the cultures and traditions of those they encountered. This impressive feat could not have been achieved by ferocity or ignorance alone. The more we learn about our northern ancestors and ancient tribes, the deeper our faith becomes. A valuable technique for improving knowledge in the realm of Norse paganism involves interpreting and reformulating the literature, poetry and prose one encounters. In addition, exploring translations of these texts into different languages can help deepen one's understanding of Norse wisdom, mythology and the wealth of ancient and forgotten knowledge contained within them. The third step on the path to becoming a practicing pagan involves making offerings to the gods. Offerings in the form of mead, wine, meat, cheese and other foods empower the gods, enabling them to provide assistance when needed. Again, emphasizing the importance of gift exchange in Norse paganism is crucial. When one offers a gift or offering to the gods, they reciprocate this act of generosity, as they draw strength from these offerings. Understanding which gifts are appropriate for each god should be part of the learning and research process. For example, Odin does not consume food but only drinks. By making offerings of meat, cheese or any other unsuitable food, we greatly reduce the likelihood of receiving help in return. Mead, on the other hand, serves as an ideal offering for Odin. Acquiring such pertinent information requires continuous reading, learning and research in the realm of Asatru. The key is to start small, using small offering bowls, composing personal sacred verses and seeking the blessings of the gods. It is critical to engage in dialogue with the gods, seeking their approval and feedback regarding the offerings provided. As you gain confidence in your ability to offer appropriately, you can gradually expand and refine your practices. While some individuals may go from offering a small bottle of mead to building hearths where they offer meat through the element of fire, it is critical not to hesitate to take these small initial steps. Begin this journey now and, in due time, you will find yourself expanding and deepening your Asatru journey.

The fourth step involves making connections with other pagans, identifying a community with the same ideology as you and engaging with it. Although Asatru is a personal religion, it also includes community practices such as ancestor veneration, collective prayer, dance and song. Participation in shared rituals, such as the consumption of consecrated mead and communal worship and invocation of the gods, assumes importance within this religious framework. Therefore, finding one's pagan lineage and becoming an integral part of it is crucial. In addition, making connections with other pagans fosters a better understanding of one's faith and facilitates the deepening of personal beliefs. Being part of a support group of like-minded individuals proves immensely helpful in conducting research related to one's religion. Moreover, when other adherents share their experiences, one realizes the similarities between one's own encounters and those of others. This sense of shared identity strengthens faith and enables one to confidently counter arguments that question the existence of gods. Such individuals possess an unwavering acceptance of the divine presence, strengthened by the knowledge that other devotees have had similar experiences. The fifth step to follow diligently in Norse paganism involves embracing fun and pleasure. Again, it is crucial to remember that gods and goddesses are similar to friends and family. There is no need to ask forgiveness for transgressions or to express excessive sorrow. Instead, one can approach them as one would a trusted friend or respected elder within one's family, sharing their problems and seeking guidance and wisdom. Unlike many traditional religions, Asatru does not adhere to a rigid set of sacred teachings that must be accepted unconditionally.

There are no hidden mysteries or secrets reserved only for masters or prophets. All the necessary information is readily available in folklore and primary sources, accessible to anyone who is willing to read and interpret according to their own knowledge and spirituality. The deities worshipped in Asatru, originally from northern Europe, embody the family and community values cherished by pagans. The primary deities, such as Odin, Frigga, Thor and Freya, belong to the same family, exemplifying the importance of kinship. Moreover, the Asatru religion's emphasis on ancestral worship further reinforces the importance of family and community ties. Ancestor veneration constitutes an integral component of this faith, as evidenced by the two main Asatru rituals, the Blot and the Sumble, both of which are closely related to honoring one's ancestors.

BELIEFS

The Asatru faith assumes that gods and goddesses are living entities, similar to human beings, with the particularity of their existence in a separate realm and possession of extraordinary powers. These divine beings actively engage in human affairs. The Asatruar believe that divine beings can be classified into different groups. One such group is the Aesir, worshipped by pagans and neopagans alike. The Aesir are commonly described as benevolent, strong, valiant and a force for good. On the other hand, the Vanir are seen as indirectly related to the Aesir group and represent aspects of creation such as nature and the earth. In addition, there are the Jotnar, who are giants who constantly oppose the Aesir. These two groups are in constant conflict, with the Jotnar symbolizing the exact opposite of the Aesir. However, there are exceptions, as some giants have cooperated with the gods and have even, in some cases, given birth to their offspring. In addition, the Asatruar believe that those who live righteous lives and die bravely in battle will be rewarded in the afterlife. These individuals are believed to be escorted by the Valkyries, led by Freyja, to a place called Valhalla. In Valhalla, the fallen warriors join Odin, the leader of the gods, and participate in a banquet with a pig called Särimner. This pig is slaughtered, consumed and then resurrected every day. Similarly, the warriors of Valhalla fight Odin daily. In contrast, cowards and the immoral are sent to a place called Hifhel, which serves as a tormenting realm for the wicked. Those who fall into neither the valiant nor the immoral category end up in a place known as Hel. It is important to note that Hel in Norse mythology differs significantly from the concept of hell in other faiths. Hel is depicted as a serene and peaceful realm, similar to limbo. The Vikings adhered to a code that governed their actions, dictating what was right and what was wrong. Modern followers of Asatru also have a similar code, guiding them to live righteous lives without succumbing to sinful behavior. Asatru is a polytheistic religion, which worships multiple gods and does not diminish the significance of other religions' gods. In contrast, Christianity recognizes a trinity consisting of God, Jesus and the Holy Spirit, seen as one supreme entity. Christians also believe in a fixed number of kingdoms ruled by one God. The Islamic faith, likewise, rejects the existence of any god other than Allah and rejects the beliefs of other religions. Consequently, Asatru does not seek to impose itself on others, and there is no desire for conquest or crusades. People can choose to follow the Asatru faith as a direct continuation of their pagan ancestors, who practiced it before the widespread conversion to Christianity. The Asatru understanding of the afterlife is not as clearly defined as in the Christian faith. While other religions envision heaven for the righteous and a fiery hell for sinners, Asatru interprets death differently. Hel in Norse paganism is simply a realm of tranquility and peace, where the deceased are not subject to torment. However, those who commit grave sins and are considered the last among the last are sent to Nastrond. This place serves as an eternal punishment for individuals who lead immoral lives and ignore the virtues outlined in the "Nine Noble Virtues." To be sentenced to Nastrond, the severity of the crime must be exceptionally high, and only the most heinous criminals, such as rapists, murderers and oath-breakers, are sentenced to suffer in this realm.

THE NINE NOBLE VIRTUES OF ASATRU

The Nine Noble Virtues, initially formulated by the Odinic Rite in England, are believed to be a contemporary concept. However, in their essence, they uphold the same principles conveyed by the ancient Norse texts. Moreover, they encapsulate more than just the ideals esteemed by the Norse people of antiquity, transcending into a flexible framework for individual conduct and decision-making throughout life. More importantly, these virtues provide guidance on how to deal with the consequences of one's actions.

1 SELF-RELIANCE

Waiting for things to happen without making sacrifices or relying on others is not logical. Instead, we should depend on ourselves and devote time and effort to meet our own needs. Asatru is a religion that values this virtue as it seeks to help people become strong and stable in their lives and in their own spiritual journey. By having self-confidence, Asatru followers also learn to take responsibility for their own actions, challenges and shortcomings. Even if we are not the cause of the problem, it is ultimately our responsibility to find a solution. A self-sufficient person understands this and avoids self-pity or circumstances of blame, focusing instead on finding a solution. Regularly practicing self-reliance can greatly improve one's personal life.

2 THE TRUTH

Although it may seem strange, telling the truth can sometimes have unexpected negative outcomes. However, it can also be beneficial to our mental well-being and relationships with others. It is important to understand that there is a difference between what is universally accepted as truth and what we personally believe to be true. Before we can discuss these truths, we must learn to distinguish between them. In general, real truth is what everyone agrees on and wants to hear, while spiritual truth is what we believe deep down. Many people just share the first kind of truth because they want to fit in with their social groups.

3 SELF-DISCIPLINE

Greed was not accepted by the Norse people. At a time when resources had to be preserved and famine was a real danger, people had to be disciplined. It was not a matter of choice, but of survival. Moreover, being loyal meant having self-control. It took a lot of strength for a man to wait for the arrival of the enemy and a lot of determination for both men and women to sacrifice their lives to honor the gods. It is obvious that those who lacked self-control were not welcomed into the tribe. Thieves and traitors were expelled, imprisoned or killed and offered as sacrifices to the gods. In general, the gods and people of the past valued discipline.

4 HONOR

Being honorable means always doing what you believe is right. It is like having a compass inside you that helps you make the right choices. In Norse paganism, honor is really important and is a pillar of a person's moral values. If you don't have honor, all the other good qualities don't really count. Honor should guide you in everything you do and help you understand what is right and what is wrong. If you rely on honor, you will have a good reputation that you can be proud of. You will feel good about yourself, have strong confidence, and others will respect you.

5 HOSPITALITY

In the past, it was really important for people to be friendly and welcoming to each other, just as we are kind to our close friends and family members. The ancient Norse people were also like that. They believed a lot in respecting each other. Even though they lived far from each other, they still opened their homes to strangers and gave them a safe place to stay. We can learn from them by trying to be kind to others. Even if we cannot give people food and a place to stay like they did, we can still make someone's day better by saying something kind to them or helping them.

6 INDUSTRIOUSNESS

Just as the Norse people did not leave their fate to the gods, it is crucial that individuals understand the importance of exerting diligent effort to achieve their goals. This responsibility extends not only to the Norse gods, but also to one's community, loved ones, and, most importantly, oneself. In ancient times, physical labor was essential for sustenance. Although modern society offers alternative means of earning a living, the need to work hard remains unchanged to achieve desired results. The pursuit of certain goals often requires considerable effort and time. However, with perpetual determination, any obstacle can be overcome. Although various strategies can be adopted, it is essential to avoid vacillation and instead proceed steadfastly toward the ultimate goal.

7 PERSEVERANCE

In the lives of the Norse pagans, it was really important never to give up, even when things were difficult and complicated. They had to undertake long and arduous journeys by sea, and sometimes there was not enough food for everyone. They also had to protect their tribe from enemies who wanted to harm them. Surely their determination to keep going and not give up helped them to find new ideas, and to grow and improve. The same determination also helped the Saxons, fighting against a great invader named Charlemagne. Unfortunately, this led to a very sad event called the Verden Massacre, where many Saxons lost their lives. The significant aspect is learning to suffer and understanding that not giving in to adversity is really important.

8 HONESTY

Despite being mentioned only twice in the Poetic Edda, the Norse god of truth, Foresti, is of significant importance to both pagan Norse and Asatruar. To lead a life of integrity, it is essential to behave honestly in every aspect of existence. The concept of honesty goes beyond simply telling the truth when it is convenient; rather, it requires a commitment to truthfulness regardless of prevailing circumstances. In the realm of interpersonal connections, honesty encompasses both faithfulness and truthful communication. Although difficult to embody, honesty remains an indispensable virtue for every follower of Asatru.

9 COURAGE

In Norse myths and ancient times, courage was shown through both physical and mental bravery during battles. War had great significance, as it provided opportunities to recognize and admire acts of courage and valor. Similarly, war played a crucial role in northern society, as the peoples of northern Germany relied on raiding neighboring villages and clans to survive and defend themselves against invaders. The presence of courage was essential to keep warriors united as they fought together to protect their homes and community, regardless of the unfavorable circumstances they faced. It was believed that death in battle would be rewarded with admission into Valhalla, where warriors would take part in banquets and training in preparation for Ragnarok, a final battle in which they would be destined to fight alongside Odin and the gods.

INTERACTING WITH ASATRU COMMUNITIES

An effective approach to engaging with the Asatru faith and discovering one's way is to make connections with other practitioners and pagans. Acquiring a mentor or becoming part of an Asatru community can facilitate a deeper understanding of the complexities inherent in some of the abstract principles and doctrines of this religion. In addition, such engagement fosters a sense of belonging and helps in the transition to adopting a pagan lifestyle. By immersing oneself in a supportive community, one also gains valuable companionship, an essential component in the quest for faith, which facilitates an easier process of spiritual learning and growth.

HEATHENRY

Heathenry, referred to by various other names such as paganism, Germanic neo-paganism or contemporary Germanic paganism, is a recently established religious movement. It emerged in Europe in the early 20th century and has its roots in pre-Christian beliefs followed by Germanic tribes from the Iron Age to the early Middle Ages. Paganism seeks to revive and reconstruct ancient belief systems by drawing evidence from folklore, history, and archaeology. This polytheistic belief system centered on a pantheon of gods, goddesses, and goddesses from the pre-Christian era of the Germanic regions. Adherents of this new religious movement embrace the cosmological perspectives of ancient societies and tribes, as well as the concept of animism, which posits that the natural world is inhabited by divine spirits and beings. Followers, who identify themselves as "pagans," adhere to an ethical system based on loyalty, personal integrity and honor. Beliefs regarding the afterlife vary, although this topic receives limited attention among pagans. Practitioners strive to understand and revive forgotten belief systems by consulting sources such as Old Norse texts (e.g., the Poetic Edda and Prose Edda), Old English texts such as Beowulf, German texts from the Middle Ages (e.g., the Nibelungenlied), archaeological evidence related to pre-Christian Northern Europe, and folklore-based stories known as "Lore." Pagan believers engage in sacrificial rites and rituals called "Blots," offering libations and food to their deities. Most rituals involve a ceremony known as Symbel, during which a toast is made to the gods with an alcoholic beverage. Some practitioners also engage in rituals aimed at achieving an altered state of reality and receiving wisdom from spiritual beings and unseen deities. The most popular rituals are Seiðr and Galdr. While some individuals engage in these rituals alone, others perform the ceremonies in small groups called kindreds or hearths. These group rituals typically take place in open spaces or dedicated buildings. Rather than contemplating the meaning of paganism, it is more pertinent to consider the actions and practices that must be adhered to. This faith does not impose a specific lifestyle or belief system on its adherents. Unlike other religions, it does not engage in missionary work or attempt to convert others to the faith. Although it lacks prescribed practices or scriptures, the faith upholds some key principles. Paganism predates Christianity and other religions, and is believed to have been practiced by people in northern Europe over a millennium ago. These people include Anglo-Saxons, Scandinavians, and Germans.

Although these faiths faced harsh persecution during the expansion of Christianity, their modern revival has met with minimal opposition. Modern pagan groups include Asatru and Germanic pagan reconstructionism. Asatru, also known as Odinism, has experienced significant growth in Iceland and has once again gained official recognition as a national religion.

06
NORSE PAGANISM

Norse paganism observes two primary rituals known as Blōt and Symbel. The celebrations are often organized by followers, and revolve around ceremonies to mark significant life events or to honor deities. Originally, blōt involved the sacrificial offering of animals to gain the favor of deities or pay homage to ancestors. After the sacrifice, a feast was held in which participants consumed the meat of the sacrificed animal. Blōt ceremonies were typically conducted to seek specific wishes, such as peace, favorable weather, abundant harvests or victory. In modern times, the practice of sacrificing animals has been considered inhumane by most individuals, resulting in a shift to offering food, drink or other objects to the gods. However, the tradition of concluding the ritual with a banquet remains. In outdoor blōt ceremonies, sacrificial objects are often thrown into a bonfire, while in indoor blōt ceremonies, participants reserve a place for the god or ancestor they wish to honor. Symbel is a ritual involving the use of one or two potori horns filled with mead or another appropriate beverage. Following the pagan practice of blessing and sanctifying drinks, the horns are circulated so that everyone can participate. Typically, the first round of toasts is dedicated to the gods, the second to the ancestors, and the third to the collective decision of the gathered pagans. In addition to making offerings to the gods, many pagans also leave small gifts to domestic "hidden people" who reside in their surroundings, such as goblins who live nearby. These offerings are often placed in a special bowl or on a small altar within the garden. Pagans often make a small offering to their pets when baking bread or creating mead, as a means of seeking good luck and dispelling negative energies that might affect their products. It is important to show respect toward one's pet spirit and honor its personal space, which can be achieved by maintaining a clean home environment. Effort to maintain positive relationships with hidden people is always encouraged.

PAGAN MORALITY AND ETHICS

Although the term "pagan" has always been associated with incivility and immorality, followers of this religious tradition oppose such stereotypes. Pagans ground their ethical and moral principles in the behaviors exhibited by characters in the ancient Norse sagas. Their ethical framework focuses on the concepts of honor, hospitality, diligence, courage and honesty, while also emphasizing the importance of family ties. Within the pagan community, individuals are expected to keep their commitments, particularly those made under oath, because of a strong emphasis on personal responsibility.

The community commonly espouses the belief that one's actions define one's character. In contrast to conventional notions of sin, most pagan practitioners reject the idea that assigning blame for past actions is beneficial, arguing that it is more harmful than constructive.

THE BLOT

The Blot ceremony holds significant importance within the Asatru tradition. The ritual begins with a formal consecration according to a specific formula. In addition, a crucial element at the beginning of the blot ritual involves the declaration of a truce and the establishment of peace among all members present. At the end of this ceremony, verses from the poetic Edda are recited. Next, participants engage in the passage of a potentory horn, where they offer toasts and consume drinks in honor of the gods and ancestors. Libations are also offered to the worshipped deities. The initial part of the ritual commonly takes place outdoors, followed by a communal feast that generally takes place indoors. This feast is accompanied by various forms of entertainment, such as music and dance.

Four Blot ceremonies exist throughout the year, including:

- *The Jolablot or Yuleblot at the winter solstice - The special event on this day is the lighting of candles by children to celebrate the rebirth of the Sun.*
- *The Sigurblot or Victory ritual on the first day of summer.*

- *The Sumarblot or summer ritual during the Summer Solstice.*
- *The Veturnattablot or winter night ritual on the first day of winter.*

In addition to the above primary rituals, there are additional practices, such as the Gooar, that are conducted on an individual basis, as well as localized rituals tailored for smaller communities. Interestingly, all rituals and ceremonies organized by the Asatru Association, including their weekly meetings, are accessible to the general public.

THE SUMBLE

The Sumble, originally a Saxon ritual, has been adopted by modern Norse pagans. It usually follows the Veizla and is a ceremonial event. Tacitus mentions this ritual in his work -Germany-, expressing surprise at tribe members openly discussing their personal matters before the entire community. The Sumble is also mentioned in other literary works, including Heimskringla, Beowulf, and the Jómsvíkinga saga. During a Sumble, there are three additional roles besides the regular participants: the Drighten, the Thule, and the Valkyrie. The Drighten is responsible for overseeing the Sumble and declaring its start and turns. The Thule acts as the guardian of the community's and the participants' fortunes, defying any oath or boast that might harm fortune or offend the gods. If a participant is challenged, he or she has the opportunity to restate his or her claim and may request support from any of those present. However, it is important to note that challenges should not be taken personally, as the goal of Thule is to protect the örlög (destiny) and fortune of the group. If the challenged individual does not keep the oath or if his or her statement is false, the Thule emphasizes that the group has warned the gods, placing the blame solely on the challenged individual rather than the group. The Valkyrie, typically a woman, blesses the drink and is responsible for pouring at least the first mug because she believes women possess magical qualities of nourishment and healing. According to tradition, any boast, oath or toast made during a Sumble is believed to reach the gods directly through the Well of the Wyrd. Participants are expected to take their words seriously, as they have the power to influence the Wyrd, positively or negatively. To maintain the sacredness of the event and separate it from everyday life, Sumble are performed in closed rooms that exist outside of everyday space and time. This setting fosters a connection between participants, deities, ancestors and the spirit world. The structure and timing of Sumble festivals vary depending on the content of the rituals. Usually, the first part of the ceremony, is dedicated to gods and spirits, the second to heroes and ancestors, and the third is open to oaths and toasts. Additional rounds may follow, often involving performances of song and poetry. At the end of each round the remaining drink is poured into a hlautbolli. A portion is taken from the bowl with a ladle, which is then poured back into the drinking horn. The horn is refilled with more blessed drink and the round continues. This ritual allows for the sharing of drinks among gods, ancestors and mortals. Regardless of the number of rounds, it is crucial to remember these important aspects:

- *Sumble is a sacred ceremony that needs to preserve its solemn atmosphere, rather than turning into a mere social gathering.*
- *It is considered inappropriate not to pay full attention to those holding the drinking horn during a Sumble.*
- *Interruptions, comments, initiating irrelevant conversations or shouting are considered highly rude.*
- *Getting drunk during the Sumble is also considered very rude and to be avoided.*
- *All participants are expected to pay full attention to each toast and to respond with the word "Hail" after drinking.*
- *If a participant cannot take part in the drinking ritual, he or she may choose to kiss the side of the horn. This act will not be perceived in any way as peculiar or out of the ordinary.*

Bragarfull, also known as "cup of promise," "head cup," or "best cup," was a traditional Scandinavian ritual involving drinking from a cup or horn, during which individuals made solemn vows while drinking from the cup, which circulated among the participants.

PROFESSION

The ceremony described is a significant event in the Asatru tradition, serving as a declaration of faith and a crucial moment in an individual's life. It signifies a new understanding of life and self, and although it is a short and simple ceremony, its sacredness and importance cannot be underestimated. Usually conducted during a regular meeting or in conjunction with a blot, this ceremony aims to actively engage an individual with the Asatru faith. It is essential that the "profession" ceremony be done in a place of authentic faith, after deep introspection and prayer. After performing the ritual, any previous religious affiliation or identity is dropped, emphasizing a complete departure from other belief systems. Those who do not fully understand this concept are advised to postpone the event until they feel adequately prepared to connect with the gods. It is important to note that there is no pressure or coercion in the act of professing, as it remains a voluntary choice of the individual. Coercive or insincere professions undermine deep commitment to both community and faith. Asatru rituals are inclusive for all, regardless of whether one has performed the ceremonial profession. Next, a nine-round Sumbel ceremony is typically conducted, with each round dedicated to one of the nine core values of Asatru.

TALISMANS

A runic talisman, alternatively referred to as an amulet, is a physical object or pendant containing a rune that individuals can carry with them. The specific rune or combination of runes embedded in the talisman determines its potential effects. They can promote good fortune, ensure safe travel, promote prosperity or provide protection against malevolent forces and bad luck. Talismans can be worn as jewelry such as necklaces or rings, attached to purses as key chains, displayed on altars or in nearby places, kept in pockets or wallets, or presented as gifts. The method for creating a talisman depends on the intended purpose and intentions of the individual.

CREATING A TALISMAN

The creation of a talisman includes various methods and guidelines, which depend on an individual's personal beliefs and religious practices. For example, followers of Odinism may choose to fashion their talisman on Wednesday, a day revered by followers of Odin. Some individuals may recite sacred oaths or passages during the creation process, while others may choose to create their talisman within a sacred space adorned with crystals or Epsom salt. In addition, timing has significance in this endeavor. To amplify and attract magical energy, it is advisable to create the talisman during the waxing moon, while during the waning moon it is advisable to ward off negative energies or malevolence. The following steps outline the basic instructions for talisman creation, with additional choices regarding sacred bonds influenced solely by personal beliefs.

- In the initial stages of talisman creation, the main step is to obtain the desired material for engraving. This material may include various materials such as wood, stone, paper, parchment, bone, horn, leather, clay or shells. While remaining flexible in your choice of material, it is advisable to opt for natural materials since they come directly from the Earth. This preference increases the magical power of the talisman due to their inherent organic nature.

- When deciding to use wood, people may find that using softwood varieties such as pine or fir is more advantageous than hardwood species such as maple or birch because of their reduced likelihood of cracking and splitting. In addition, the way the wood is obtained should be considered. Some individuals believe that causing damage to any living plant is morally questionable, thus opting to use dead branches, which offer the same effectiveness. Conversely, others believe that requesting permission and acknowledging the sacrifice of the tree is an integral part of the ritual. Ultimately, the method of wood procurement depends on each individual's personal beliefs, as long as it does not involve the reckless destruction of living organisms solely for one's own benefit.

- After selecting the appropriate material, it is important to consider the purpose behind the creation of a talisman.

Thought should be given to the intended function it should serve, such as whether it is intended to be a keychain to attach to a suitcase or backpack, for example. In such cases, it would be advisable to incorporate the Raidho rune, known for its association with safe and successful travel. Alternatively, if one imagines the talisman to be a pendant designed to aid a sick acquaintance in healing, the use of the Uruz rune, known for its connotations of health and vigor, would be helpful in facilitating the healing process.

- Understanding the purpose behind the creation of a talisman is critical to selecting the most appropriate runes to incorporate. Before carving the talisman, it is advisable to make a rough draft on paper to avoid damaging the talisman due to lack of practicality. This precaution is especially important when multiple runes are used, resulting in the formation of a binding rune, in which several runes are combined into a single design. It should be emphasized that the design of the bindruna, that is, a design that combines several runes into one, is entirely at the discretion of the individual. Further insight on this topic can be obtained from the section Binding Runes.

- One may choose to create a bindruna that incorporates one's name, emphasizing the importance of using one's authentic name, regardless of whether it is one's first name, full name or initials. The name chosen should be the one that resonates most strongly with personal identity, even if it is a nickname or a name associated with their pagan beliefs. In this way, the talisman becomes deeply personalized to the individual. Conversely, if the bindruna is intended for another person, you will create it using their name. Before engraving the talisman, it is advisable to first transcribe the name in runic symbols and practice writing them on paper. Once the exercise is completed, it is advisable to destroy the test rune.

- After completing the design, the next step is to ensure its durability. The choice of material determines the method by which the talisman can be engraved. For example, if you use wood, you have the option of carving, burning or painting the design. However, it is important to note that burning is not suitable for paper or parchment materials.

- Various tools can be used: such as a wood burning kit, dremel, knife, brush, pen or marker, or any other suitable tool, depending on the material you will have chosen.

- During the process of carving your talisman, direct your attention to the powers associated with your selected runes. It is advisable to consider this effort as a ceremonial event, where you can engage in incense burning, music playing, chanting or any other practice that promotes spiritual connection. It is worth noting that the ancient Norse belief system includes animism, according to which all elements of the natural world possess spiritual entities. Such entities include rivers, mountains, grass, trees and all other components found in nature. Therefore, it is advisable to express gratitude toward the spirits inherent in wood or stone materials by acknowledging their existence and expressing appreciation for their permission to use them.

- The belief among ancient Norse cultures was that the incorporation of red in rune markings served as a symbol of blood and sacrifice, as blood was believed to enhance the spiritual forces within the rune. Some individuals choose to use their own blood to decorate the rune, ensuring its exclusivity and personal connection. Alternatively, paint may be used as a dye, with shades of red, green or blue more in keeping with the natural environment, although other colors may be used depending on the extent to which one adheres to traditional practices.

- After the talisman is dry, it can be coated with shellac or clear varnishes to preserve its durability. In addition, the talisman can be embellished with other natural components such as crystals or feathers. In the case of a necklace, a chain or cord can be incorporated.

- The completion of the talisman requires its recharging or activation through magical means. In accordance with the inscription on the talisman, various methods can be employed: such as reciting the names of runes, invoking deities or harnessing the spiritual energy inherent in them, burning incense or candles, using the energy emitted by crystals, or engaging in any other practice of spiritual connection. By firmly grasping the talisman and directing one's concentration toward the intended power and desired energies to be infused into the object, the charging process can be effectively carried out.

- To increase the power of the talisman, it is advisable to place it inside a cloth by wrapping a rope around the talisman with nine turns. Afterwards, the talisman should be hidden in darkness, thus recalling the gestation period and the subsequent "birth" of the talisman. The duration of this recharging process should be observed in multiples of nine, such as nine days, nine hours and nine minutes. Alternatively, placing the talisman under the brightness of the full moon or within the confines of a crystal grid can also facilitate its recharging.

- Once the talisman has fulfilled its intended function or reached the end of its usefulness, it is essential to dispose of it by burning or burying it in order to effectively relinquish its magical properties.

ALTARS

Not all individuals own an altar; however, a significant number of pagans maintain a structure within their residences where they can focus their attention while communicating with deities. An altar includes several objects that have personal significance to its creator. It should not be conceived as adhering to specific or conventional objects; rather, it should exclusively accommodate the elements that bring comfort and resonance to the individual. Essentially, an altar is a self-made or curated space composed exclusively of objects that evoke a sense of comfort and familiarity. Two main types of altars are used within pagan practices: indoor altars and outdoor altars.

INDOOR ALTARS

An indoor altar offers greater flexibility in terms of placement. For people who have a strong attachment to family heirlooms and wish to display them on their altar, an indoor setting offers greater security than an outdoor altar where these items could be at risk of damage or theft by animals. In addition, an indoor altar allows for the inclusion of items that would otherwise perish outdoors. The creation of an indoor altar depends on the preferred method of communicating with spirits. For example, people who practice runic meditation may find it meaningful to place their own set of runes on the altar. In addition, depictions of favorite gods or multiple deities can be incorporated in the form of pictures, drawings or paintings. Rocks, plants and objects related to spiritual rituals, such as drinking horns, can also be added to the altar. In cases where interaction with gods and spirits is facilitated through the consumption of food and drink, objects related to this practice may be included on the altar. Drinking horns, particularly those finely carved from cow horns, are particularly popular among Ásatrúar practitioners. One may also consider placing a plate on the altar for the purpose of offering objects to the gods and spirits. While many home altars focus on ancestors rather than gods and spirits, people often choose to display photographs of their family and deceased ancestors on the altar. Items that once belonged to loved ones are also hung on the altar, facilitating communication with long-lost ancestors. The belief that the dead continue to exist in our memories, our hearts and our environment is emphasized by most pagans, surpassing any notion of an afterlife or realm of death beyond the mortal world. This belief ensures that our ancestors never really leave us. In my home we have a family altar that honors the ancestors and significant spirits of our collective families. On this altar we display important objects, including photographs of our grandparents and great-grandparents. We also incorporate flowers, wood carvings, ritual tools used in ceremonies, gifts and offerings to deities and spirits, among various other items. Ultimately, the selection of items to include on an altar depends on the preferred method of communication with gods, spirits and ancestors.

OUTDOOR ALTARS

An outdoor altar differs in some characteristics from an indoor one. Although not everyone is fortunate enough to reside in an area conducive to having an outdoor altar, those who have the opportunity may opt for it. The advantage of an outdoor altar lies in the ability to pour libations directly onto the ground to deities and spirits. Individuals can create a dedicated ritual space that is aesthetically pleasing, such as by incorporating it into their garden. Many devotees, as beautification, incorporate trees and occasionally a pond. Others use a large rock as a platform on which to place objects intended for deities and spirits, while some build altars using rocks of various sizes. A common practice is to enclose the area around the altar with a circle, often bounded by smaller rocks, wooden sticks, fences or ropes. Although ancient narratives do not explicitly describe indoor altars, some offer suggestions as to how outdoor sacred spaces were established. A type of sacred place called a vé is mentioned in the Icelandic sagas. The vé denotes a sacred space delineated by vébönds, which are bonds or chains attached to hazel sticks. In addition, several stories describe the presence of specific rocks, boulders, ponds, lakes and streams, which served as focal points for personal rituals.

07
THE RUNES

THE HISTORY OF RUNES

The term "rune" comes from the Old English word "rún," meaning secret or mystery. It is also related to the Old High German word "rune," meaning a secret conversation or whisper. In addition, the word "rune" can be found in Old Norse as "rúnir" or "rúnar," which carries the meaning of magical signs and hidden magic. The use of runes can be traced back to the Germanic peoples, who employed them from at least the second century B.C. until the Middle Ages. However, extensive linguistic research suggests that the word is found in various geographical regions with similar meanings. It is plausible to assume that the concept of rune is ancient and does not correspond exclusively to the physical artifacts of past history. The notion of rune dates back to the Indo-European family tree and existed among the ancestors of our ancestors. Over the years, more than 6,000 runic inscriptions have been discovered, with the highest concentrations found in northern European regions. This fact disproves the myth that runes originated from

Mediterranean writing, a theory that practitioners of the Asatru faith should abandon for good. If this theory were true, one would expect to find a greater concentration of runes near the southern Mediterranean civilizations. The term "Futhark" is derived from the first six letters of the runic alphabet. The runes are: F (Fehu), U (Uruz), Th (Thurisaz), A (Ansuz), R (Raidho), and K (Kenaz). But more on this later. The Anglo-Saxon, Norse, and Icelandic runic systems are remnants of the various runic systems used by the peoples of the North. Although they share similarities, they also show some differences. Over time, the significance of the Ancient Futhark runes was lost for a variety of reasons. Futhark was rediscovered in 1865 by Sophus Bugge, a Norwegian philologist and linguist. The original runic alphabet consisted of twenty-four runes arranged in three rows of eight runes. Later, Norway and Denmark reduced this pattern to a system of only sixteen runes, while the English Saxons expanded it to thirty-three runes in some cases. Despite these changes, the Runemasters continued to work with the original twenty-four runes. They may have used later pictograms, but the runic powers remained the same. Any attempt to change the order of the Futhark is likely to be misleading, since the ancient order possesses magical precision. The Futhark consists of twenty-four runes arranged in three rows of eight runes. Each row is known as Aett or Airt. For our purposes, we will consider the Ancient Futhark as a collection of traditional codes or magical characters (galdr) that facilitate the circulation of information between the earthly and otherworldly realms. The real secret of the runes lies in understanding the meta-knowledge underlying their arrangement, a knowledge that permeates the runic system. For example, Jera, the Yrune, meaning "year," occupies the twelfth position in the Ancient Futhark. Is this a mere coincidence? This knowledge has been lost over time and Asatru seeks to recover it. The origin of the runes can be traced back to the Germanic peoples of the 1st and 2nd centuries CE, a period characterized by linguistic similarities with the Common Germanic era. These runes were later adapted for use in numerous other languages, including Danish, English, Gothic, Norwegian, Hebrew, Icelandic, Lithuanian, German, and Russian. The Semitic languages derived from trade interactions with Silk Road traders known as Khazari. Runes can be read right to left or left to right, which contributes to the challenge of translating the various meanings. However, historical inscriptions have been discovered and translated by contemporary experts, greatly helping to attribute meaning to the runes. Runes themselves are symbols that can be written or engraved on various materials, such as stone, wood or paper, and are believed to possess the magical power to attract love, money, friendship and success. From a scientific point of view, determining the age of runes is challenging. Some researchers claim that they have existed for more than 3,000 years, while most scientists agree that they are no more than 2,000 years old. Mythologically, runes are considered a gift from Odin, who acquired wisdom by hanging on the tree of life for nine days and nights. He then transmitted this knowledge to human beings. Runes were mainly used as a magical alphabet, for purposes of divination and fortune-telling, and for the creation of talismans and amulets called "bindrune". These artifacts combine two or three different runes to form a powerful magical talisman. In ancient times they were essential items for the people of the North, including the Vikings and the people of the British Isles. The rest of Northern Europe also used runes, such as the Druids who used them in magical rituals to achieve victory in battle, bountiful harvests and more. Ancient Futhark symbols continue to be used for divination and the creation of talismans. Studying runic magic can attract work, love and friendship, success in business, material and spiritual wealth, health and more. If you are looking for an interesting and mysterious system of magic, runes is the best place to start.

USING RUNES

Runes originated as a form of written communication and continue to be of significant importance in the realm of Norse language. It is very likely that, as a reader of this text, you possess some familiarity with the concept of runes. If not, I will attempt to give you the tools to understand the basics and beyond. As discussed earlier, runes, runic writing and runic language have long fascinated the imaginations of individuals throughout history. This group of enthusiasts includes esteemed figures such as shamans, wandering sages and famous divine kings, including Odin, the revered deity of Norse mythology. In various ancient cultures, runes were used to increase the power of amulets, jewelry and weapons carried by warriors in battle. These inscriptions were believed to confer protective and magical properties on the wearer. Some warriors, such as the legendary berserkers, even adorned their bodies with runic tattoos, believing that these markings would grant them invincibility against sword blows and arrow wounds. Runes were also engraved on tombs and colossal standing stones, serving as a commemoration of extraordinary people or achievements, as well as guiding spirits into the afterlife. In addition, runes were recited and chanted as components of magical spells, and were engraved on landmarks that supposedly possessed the ability to foretell the future. Even the Nazis, who came to power in Germany before World War II, showed a fascination with runes and the supernatural powers that could come from deciphering their meanings. Currently, runes continue to be interpreted in popular culture, particularly in fantasy literature and movies such as The Lord of the Rings, the Harry Potter series, and in video games such as The Elder Scrolls: Skyrim. An interesting observation concerning these cases is the consistent association of runes with mystical meaning. Even in contemporary stories and works of fiction, we are inclined to attribute at least some degree of magical power to these enigmatic symbols of humanity's historical past. Whether they possess real supernatural abilities, are used as symbols and amulets, or have the ability to foretell the future or access the past, runes have consistently enchanted the minds of those who encounter them. Unfortunately, the enduring popularity of runes has also led to considerable confusion and misinformation, both unintentional and deliberate. As a result, numerous popular assumptions regarding the nature, meaning, and potential uses of runes have been distorted due to the passage of time and historical events. In addition, the interpretation of some symbols, such as the infamous swastika, has become almost universally associated with absolute evil and human cruelty, deviating considerably from its original meaning. In Germanic runology, distinct runes represented specific letters of the alphabet and could also be used to represent entire words. The understanding of runes is closely related to language itself, as our understanding of language has evolved along with our understanding of these ancient symbols. In addition, runes can be used as a means of communicating with the deceased. However, engaging in this practice is very challenging and controversial, and caution and willingness to learn is advised. It is crucial to seek advice from someone experienced in the use of runes before attempting such endeavors, as they can result in complications or, in most cases, not produce results if one does not have sufficient experience with these symbols. In conclusion, runes possess considerable power and can offer people who believe in them insights into various aspects of their lives or, in rare cases, facilitate communication with deceased loved ones to whom they have not been able to say goodbye. To truly grasp the complexity of runes, one will benefit from delving into their various facets.

THE RUNIC ALPHABET

Each individual rune possesses a distinct and specific meaning, as clarified in the following explanation (Gronitz, n.d.). However, it is important to note that while contemporary practices often associate colors with each rune, this was not a prevalent aspect in ancient Norse magical traditions.

FEHU

Name: Fehu, "cattle." Phoneme: F. Meaning: wealth.

Symbolizes livestock, which was commonly associated with wealth at that time. However, when used for divinatory purposes, it conveys a desire for power, control, new beginnings and prosperity. This could refer to monetary resources or financial credit, as opposed to material goods such as land. According to Gronitz (n.d.), this rune confers the ability to acquire wealth and the ability to preserve it.

URUZ ᚢ

Name: Uruz, "aurochs." Phoneme: U. Meaning: willpower.

Symbolizes a wild ox. It embodies a rune of great power, similar to Fehu, but its influence cannot be possessed or manipulated. When cast, it indicates the potential nearness of individual realization. It was employed in the making of pendants and talismans with healing properties.

THURISAZ ᚦ

Name: Thurisaz, "Giant." Phoneme: Th. Meaning: danger, suffering.

It represents a thorn and possesses the ability to show passive resistance to conflict. Functioning as a protective rune, it signals impending and unforeseen alteration. Also, acting as a defensive mechanism, it protects against adversaries of all kinds.

HAGALAZ ᚺ

Name: Hagalaz, "hello." Phoneme: H. Meaning: destruction, chaos.

Represents hail. This rune refers to problematic situations that will eventually flow smoothly, just as a hailstone melts and goes away. Although it may indicate challenges or adversity, it also signifies the ability to overcome them.

ANSUZ ᚠ

Name: Ansuz, "an Aesir god." Phoneme: A. Meaning: prosperity, vitality.

Symbolizes the concept of the mouth or divine breath. It takes on the meaning of the establishment of stability and order. This rune denotes the intellectual and divine breath that permeates all aspects of creation.

RAIDHO ᚱ

Name: Raidho, "journey on horseback." Phoneme: R. Meaning: movement, work, growth.

Raidho translates as wheel or ride. When thrown, its meaning is to focus energy at the right place and time to achieve desired goals. It indicates movement, change, work.

KENAZ <

Name: Kenaz, "flashlight." Phoneme: K. Meaning: knowledge, learning.

Kenaz, or "k," represents a flashlight. When thrown, it is seen as a rune for learning, understanding, knowledge and teaching. Something that can enable greater clarity.

GEBO ✕

Name: Gebo, "gift." Phoneme: G. Meaning: generosity.

Gebo is a special symbol and represents a gift. When you throw it, it means you are connecting with someone, showing them honor and exchanging something. You are giving them a blessing and thanking the gods for the gift of life.

WUNJO ᚹ

Name: Wunjo, "joy." Phoneme: W. Meaning: joy, ecstasy.

Wunjo means joy. When cast, it reveals Wunjo, showing that even in a messy, confused world there can be balance and people can work together. It also means that positive events will happen in the future. If Wunjo shows up in a reading, it means that something good and important will happen soon.

NAUTHIZ ᚾ

Name: Nauthiz, "need." Phoneme: N. Meaning: need, unfulfilled desire.

Nauthiz symbolizes pain, which does not originate from the body, but from the spirit and then affects the mind and physical self. It is about the deep suffering that results from a "lack" during a phase of one's existence. It can also be read as the revelation of an obstacle to the possibility of fulfilling our desires.

ISA ᛁ

Name: Isa, "ice." Phoneme: I. Meaning: Suggestion.

The symbol represents ice. It is usually seen as a sign to pause a certain activity until a change occurs. But, just like melting ice, the symbol can also be liberating.

JERA ᛃ

Name: Jera, "year." Phoneme: Germanic J, modern English Y. Meaning: harvest, reward.

Jera represents a harvest, a season. When cast it shows the process of life and the significance of following the natural order of things rather than going against it to achieve desired goals.

EIHWAZ

Name: Eihwaz, "badger." Phoneme: E. Meaning: strength, stability.

Eihwaz sounds like "eo" or "æ" and represents the badger. Its meaning is that of protector and magical assistant, and it is believed to show that after something ends, something new begins.

PERTHRO

Name: Perthro. Phoneme: P. Meaning: uncertainties.

Represents the cup used to hold dice. When thrown, it symbolizes the unpredictable nature of life and the choices we make. It can be used to remember events and to help find solutions to problems.

ALGIZ

Name: Algiz (Elk). Phoneme: Z. Meaning: protection from enemies, defense of what one loves.

With a double "zz" sound, Algiz represents the moose. When thrown it means protection, defense and power. It is used to protect people and property.

SOWULO ᛋ

Name: Sowulo, "sunshine." Phoneme: S. Meaning: success, consolation.

It represents the sun and its meaning. When cast, it refers to light in the darkness and the ability to see things more clearly.

TEIWAZ ↑

Name: Teiwaz, "the god Teiwaz." Phoneme: T. Meaning: victory, honor.

Teiwaz is the creator; when this rune is cast, it promises us success without great personal sacrifice, even in the area of justice if we are in the right.

BERKANA ᛒ

Name: Berkana, "birch." Phoneme: B. Meaning: fertility, growth, sustenance.

Stands for tree or birch twig. It represents a new beginning and when cast symbolizes a birth full of power and prosperity.

EHWAZ ᛖ

Name: Ehwaz, "horse." Phoneme: E. Meaning: trust, faith, companionship.

Ehwaz sounds like "eh" and, in the literal alphabet, represents the word horse. When cast, this rune expresses the meaning that there must be a natural flow to be successful. It gives strength and the means to pursue an achievement in any field.

MANNAZ ᛗ

Name: Mannaz, "man." Phoneme: M. Meaning: increase, support.

Mannaz sounds like the letter "m" and represents man. It depicts different powers when thrown. It can reveal that we can achieve full success in life, and enable us to have the upper hand in disagreements and disputes.

LAGUZ ᛚ

Name: Laguz. Phoneme: L. Meaning: the formless, chaos, potentiality, the unknown.

Laguz sounds like "l" and represents water or a lake. When cast, the power and flow of water flows into ourselves in order to fully reach our abilities and potential.

INGWAZ

Name: Ingwaz, "the god Ingwaz." Phoneme: Ng. Meaning: the fertilization, the beginning of something, the actualization of potential.

Inguz is a "ng" sound and literally represents the idea of fertility. The meaning of the rune is to propagate our energy. It manifests the protection of homes, and the concept that we should use wisdom to increase our power over time and then use it when needed.

DAGAZ

Name: Dagaz, "day." Phoneme: D. Meaning: hope, happiness.

Dagaz sounds like the letter "d" and means day. Its meaning represents opposites, a kind of yin/yang; antithetical concepts such as those between light and dark or day and night. It restrains harmful energy, and allows good energy to pass through.

OTHALA ᛟ

Name: Othala, "inheritance." Phoneme: O. Meaning: inheritance, tradition, nobility.

Othala, which sounds like a long "o," means ancestral and sacred home or land. It is a rune representing wealth and prosperity. Othala represents wealth of friends, family and heritage. It also reveals a current state of existence and its maintenance over time. (Gronitz, n.d.)

08
FUNDAMENTALS OF DIVINATION

RUNES IN DIVINATION

Magic is often associated with the Norse people, the Vikings, and pagans in general. However, the term "pagan" actually refers to someone who does not believe in the prevailing deities of his or her time. This oversimplified definition may be why magic scares people, as the general population tends to fear anything they do not know or understand. Anything peculiar or supernatural is often perceived as magical. Interestingly, those who reject magic and claim it does not exist would readily accept it as science if it were proven. Therefore, it is crucial to keep an open mind when considering magic as a whole, as faith is the first and most crucial step. When contemplating the Vikings and their pantheon of gods, it is common to imagine human sacrifice and suffering. However, it was believed that the gods worshipped by these people were forgiving and benevolent beings who cared for and loved their followers. Contrary to popular belief, the magic and divination they practiced focused on performing good deeds, such as protecting their families and guiding the deceased to a better afterlife. Odin, the most revered and beloved god, demonstrated immense courage and selflessness by sacrificing himself and hanging himself from a tree for three days. In return, he gained knowledge of the Viking Runes, the most powerful form of magic known to mankind. These runes held the power of the universe, which Odin shared with his people upon returning to Earth. Thus, it is understandable why the Norse had such a granitic faith in the runes. Aside from their significance in social and intellectual progress, the emotional intensity they evoked among users is evident when examining the achievements of the Viking Age and the overall growth of the Norse people. Undoubtedly, they had a profound impact on those who sincerely believed in them. The reason why contemporary skeptics easily dismiss the runes is mainly due to their lack of faith. As mentioned earlier, the human mind possesses immense power, and when it focuses on something as powerful as runes and divination, the possibilities become limitless. Unfortunately, fear of the opinions or reactions of others often prevents us from experiencing extraordinary things. However, if you truly open your mind to all possibilities, every result will be magical, regardless of personal interpretation. Outside influences should never dictate one's beliefs. This mindset guided our ancestors through the darkest times, when magic and spells illuminated their world. Another crucial aspect to understand is that the ancient rune masters were probably the only literate individuals in their villages. Education was considered secondary to physical strength and battle scars. However, when a rune master read or wrote runic writing, it fascinated people, highlighting the need to see these topics through the lens of those times. For the most part, the stories of the deities or detailed explanations of each rune and its powers were beyond comprehension. In modern times, they would probably attribute these feats to trickery or deliberate manipulation. Runes were engraved or painted on various materials to bring good luck, protection and safety to families. When a warrior returned unharmed from battle and found his family safe, it was seen as a testament to the effectiveness of his power. The magic was undeniable. The use of runes in divination constitutes a crucial aspect of Norse magic, intimately linked to the runic alphabet and Viking history. In light of this, we explored the origins of this magic and the significant role runes play in galdr, one of the primary forms of ancient Scandinavian magic. Galdr specifically uses the symbols of the runic alphabet for divinatory purposes. We have thoroughly explored the runic alphabet, studying its literal meaning, sound and magical significance in the context of divination. We explored the various techniques and methods of casting runes and conducting runic readings. Just like the ancient Norse rune masters, we can draw on our inner intuition and wisdom to use these symbols for divination. Divination includes not only the runes themselves, but also their arrangement, whether it is a single rune or a group of three or more. Especially significant is the complete reading of 24 runes, often performed at the beginning of a new year. Aside from the arrangement, there are three main methods of casting runes. The first involves throwing them randomly on the ground or on a cloth. The second method involves reading only the upright runes, leaving out the inverted ones, or interpreting both orientations. The third approach involves keeping the runes in a bag, formulating the question or situation at hand, and selecting the runes individually to form the desired pattern. Rune stones can be purchased or personally engraved on various materials, such as wood, stone or crystal, as was customary during ancient Norse times. It is also common to create personal talismans or pendants with engraved runes or to incorporate them into candles. Historically, runes were used both as a traditional alphabet and for divinatory purposes. Skilled rune masters cast and interpreted runes, often casting them on cloth or on the ground as they sought the guidance of the Norse gods. Their gaze to the heavens ensured an unbiased reading, free of personal influence. In the early days, runes were not interpreted backwards. A more contemporary approach to reading runes involves extracting each stone individually from a bag, guided by intuition and selective impulses. The practice and use of runes is prevalent in the Asatru faith and is the most important form of magic within the belief system. But what exactly are runes and how do they contribute to the faith? In essence, runes are alphabetic symbols that serve as the language of the cosmos, enabling the interpretation of otherworldly messages. The journey to understanding and interpreting runes is challenging, and often leads to profound self-transformation. It is essential to approach all forms of magic with respect, reverence and caution, as runes possess the power to have a significant impact on our lives. Within the modern Asatru faith, runes serve predominantly as tools for divination, allowing practitioners to connect with their subconscious on a deep level. Engaging in runic practices can foster inner strength and confidence. It is important to clarify that runic divination does not provide lottery numbers; instead, it offers insight into one's past, present and potential future. It may also reveal a long-sought path. This interpretation of divination stems from the belief that the forces of our destiny can be examined and interpreted to discover our future to some extent. Since our actions shape our future, altering our actions in response to predicted events can lead to a change in that future. A common method of interpreting runes involves drawing three runes, representing the past, present and future. By examining these three aspects and their interrelationships, we believe we can gain insight into the future, within the boundaries of reason. Modern Asatru runic practices predominantly use the "Ancient Futhark," a runic alphabet composed of 24 runes. In addition to divination, runes can also be used in active magic, although this practice is less common. One approach to active runic magic involves the carving of a "binding rune," which combines multiple symbols to manifest the desired result. However, for the purposes of this discussion, our focus will be on runic divination, as it is the most common form of magic practiced in the Asatru faith. Therefore, in this section we will delve into the reading and interpretation of runes for divination purposes.

CHOOSING RUNES

There is a wide range of online sites and specialty stores that offer a wide variety of runes for sale. These runes are made from various materials such as stone, wood, amethyst and crystal. The choice of material is entirely up to you, and once you find the one that feels right for you, you will know instinctively that it is the correct solution. If you decide to create your own set of runes, it is important to make sure they are all uniform in size. It is critical to make sure that one side of each rune is flat, otherwise there may be technical problems when casting. We want to avoid causing doubt and confusion about the interpretation of the actual meaning. Proper storage of the runes is also of utmost importance, and it is common practice to store them in a drawstring closure bag, which is often provided when purchased online or in a store. However, if you choose to make your own runes, a bag of natural material or a small box will suffice. Just remember to keep them safe and easily accessible at all times. When purchasing a new set of runes, it is essential to make sure they are from the Ancient Futhark and not one of the later variants. Although the other versions may work, we have previously discussed the advantages of the Ancient Futhark, so it would be incorrect to choose a different path. Also, it is advisable not to skimp on quality. While some may perceive the runes as simple pieces of rock or wood, the cheaper versions will likely be irregular and the symbols may fade over time. Of course, if you create your own runes, there is always the risk of imperfections, but the difference is that you can easily and smoothly touch them up. There is also a deeply personal and inner aspect to creating your own runes. However, if this is not for you, rest assured that buying them from a reputable store will produce equally effective results.

CASTING RUNES

Rune divination, which commonly involves the casting of runes, is a method used to help practitioners make decisions in their lives, offering guidance and advice on how to handle problems or deal with certain situations. Although beginners may find rune divination exciting because of the possibility of glimpsing into the future, it is important to manage expectations. As mentioned earlier, this form of magic does not provide definitive answers to questions. However, there are established patterns and spreads that can be studied and experimented with. It is essential to create a calm environment and devote sufficient time to reading, as external disturbances can disrupt concentration and lead to inaccurate results. Starting this process with a clear and focused mind is essential. So after a few deep breaths, relax and clear your mind. You need to detach yourself from daily thoughts and focus exclusively on the problems or questions you want answers to. If desired, you can dedicate a silent prayer to your favorite deity. Runes should be placed on a runic cloth, and various distributions and arrangements, similar to tarot cards, can be employed. For beginners, it is advisable to start with a simple arrangement and thoroughly analyze each rune chosen. Once a fair amount of experience has been gained, more complex variations can be explored. Before placing the runes on the cloth, it is necessary to shake them inside the bag, similar to shuffling a deck of tarot cards. Like other forms of divination, rune lettyra considers past, present and personal influences to provide proper guidance. In a three-rune casting, three runes are taken out of the bag, one at a time and placed on the cloth. The first rune represents a general summary of the situation or problem, the second addresses potential obstacles that may be encountered, and the third indicates the actions necessary to overcome these obstacles and achieve the desired result. An arrangement of great interest is the arrangement of the nine runes. In Norse mythology, this number has great importance, seen almost as a magic number. For this reading, nine runes are selected and placed on the runic cloth. The placement of each rune and its direction should be carefully observed and interpreted along with past and present influences. It is important to note that each runic symbol has multiple meanings and it is therefore advisable to rely solely on the meaning provided. Instead, the overall context should be considered to form an interpretation. For example, the rune Ehwaz can mean a horse, a wheel or luck. This ambiguity requires considering other runes and personal influences to derive the true meaning. It may imply a stroke of luck during travel or symbolize determination to reach one's ultimate goal. In some cases, these multiple meanings may indicate an unexpected bonus or promotion at work. It is normal to initially encounter unsatisfactory results, as understanding runes and their meanings requires time, patience and years of study. Like any divination method, relying on one's intuition and ability to deduce is essential for a complete analysis. In addition, the orientation of a rune, whether upside down or upright, can drastically alter its meaning, similar to tarot cards. Rune stones or crystals used in rune divination should be kept in a small bag or pouch tied with string and cleaned after each reading. However, some rune sets may include blank (white) runes, and their use is subject to personal judgment. Traditional practitioners have reported that they do not use blank runes in their readings. So if you wish to eliminate them from your reading, that is fine too.

INTERPRETING RUNES

Now that we have taken a look at the practice of casting runes, it becomes apparent that the interpretation of these ancient symbols is no easy feat. Only a select few possess the ability to accurately read runes at their first encounter. Runic divination is indeed an art form that requires perseverance and dedication. Beginners are often recommended expert guidance to help them embark on their journey with the runes. In addition, there is a wide range of resources such as books, blogs and videos that can be consulted by those who wish to delve deeper into the world of runic divination. However, it must be understood that becoming proficient in deciphering these mystical symbols is a lifelong effort. The pursuit of knowledge, through continuous learning and reading, is a central tenet of the Asatru faith. Therefore, it is unwise to expect immediate answers after casting the runes. Even the most experienced practitioners of rune reading face challenges in their interpretation, sometimes taking weeks before the answers manifest. Therefore, I recommend practicing patiently and accepting the fact that runic divination is a complex and, most importantly, time-consuming art.

MEDITATION CAN HELP IN READINGS

Meditation, whether performed ceremonially or informally, is a valuable source of profound wisdom and serves as a direct channel for harnessing inner energy. In order for the vitki, or runic practitioner, to fully connect with the essence of each individual rune and the overall runic cosmology, a deep personal connection must be established. The flow of a powerful force grants the vitki great connection and constant access to a wealth of knowledge and insight. It is possible to tap into this flow during moments of reflection, providing the vitki with meaningful revelations about the mysteries of the runic realm. Engaging in meditation elevates one's level of thinking, and allows for greater sensory perception. By attuning oneself to one's surroundings, one becomes more perceptive to subtle details that would otherwise have been overlooked, thus enabling a deeper understanding of the runes. Rune meditation is a dynamic and challenging endeavor, requiring the reader to exercise control over his or her thoughts by suppressing harmful ones and guiding them along the wild path of the rune. When the mind is calm and focused, the intuition of the runes will begin to become clear to the practitioner. Rune meditation involves focusing on three main elements: the shape, the sound and the main idea of the runes. The practitioner should try to focus on any or all of these elements, pushing away negative thoughts and leaving only the symbols of the runes in his or her mind. Eventually, the rune will begin to communicate directly with the practitioner's consciousness. Ceremonial runic meditation can be complex or simple, depending on the preference and skill level of the practitioner. Preparation for meditation includes finding a quiet place, knowing a ritual invocation of protection and meditation techniques. In the initial stages of meditation, the practitioner may choose to focus on one element of the runic complex and gradually add others. It is important for the practitioner to develop a specific plan that suits their needs and abilities. They should aim to build a rich and diverse set of elements in their concentration, incorporating various magical techniques.

There are several methods of runic meditation that the practitioner can use. These techniques can be performed physically or entirely in the mind. The practitioner should look at the rune shape and gently chant the sound of the corresponding rune. It may be necessary to open the eyes from time to time to re-establish the rune shape. However, with practice, the practitioner will be able to maintain concentration without the need to open their eyes. They should maintain this internal concentration on the rune complex for at least a few seconds and aim to reach five minutes. After this period of concentration, the practitioner should enter a state of inner silence, remaining attentive and focused. During a period of deep thought and reflection, the rune message will be spoken aloud with a powerful sound. This is a sacred event in which the rune and the spiritual essence of the practitioner come together. The practitioner may choose to continue meditating as long as he or she feels connected to the rune energy. In this meditative state, the practitioner can explore different paths related to the rune and discover its secrets or connections with other runes. The possibilities are endless. When the connection is broken or the practitioner wants to end the meditation, he or she repeats a phrase such as "Now the work is done" and opens their eyes. As you become more familiar with the runes, you can try different informal meditative techniques. These meditations will bring you wisdom and inner knowledge. The process is simple: sit at a desk or table surrounded by runic symbols and cosmic patterns. Clear your mind and focus on the world of runes. Let your thoughts wander until you find a key idea, then follow it, drawing and taking notes on any insights that come to you. These notes can be a starting point for further work. After practicing runic meditation for a short time, the wisdom of the runes will begin to come to you at unexpected times. Sometimes the power of these forces can even cause physical phenomena near you! Practicing runic meditation regularly is an important part of the overall wisdom system and is rewarding for those who engage in it.

NORSE MAGIC OVER TIME

In the same way that the Germanic tribes integrated Norse magic into their daily lives, we have the opportunity to do the same in the present day. For the ancient Norse, magic was not just a mystical concept, but rather a form of knowledge that had great significance in their lives, along with their agricultural skills and valor in battle. Norse magic served as a means of understanding one's place in the world and shaping a desired life through one's willpower. It provided guidance and control, particularly during the Iron Age and Viking Age, when there were countless uncertainties. The use of magical rituals to unveil one's destiny was crucial, as it enabled them to respond honorably to any challenge and even alter the predetermined course of their lives. Therefore, Norse magic has always offered a means of exercising control and gaining understanding over one's existence. The Norse did not consider their fate to be an obstacle to free will, but rather believed that they could improve and shape their destiny to their own advantage. This perspective freed them from the uncertainty of a predetermined future, enabling them to accomplish great feats. Magic served as a tool to enhance their capabilities in this quest. Today, the practice of magic is in line with our desire for self-realization, acceptance of our circumstances and the quest for improvement. Although we now have access to medicine, modern health care and educational leadership, the allure and power of magic remain powerful. Norse magic was one of the first ways humans sought to exercise control over their lives and to recognize the larger world beyond themselves. It enabled practitioners to protect themselves from harm, effectively manage illness, and cultivate relationships, both personal and with the world. At a time when survival – whether through success in battle or in agricultural enterprises – was paramount, magic, the knowledge of skilled practitioners and faith in its healing properties united communities that were often physically isolated. Magic included not only mystical and natural wisdom, but also practical insights. The use of the runic alphabet, for example, expanded as a means of invoking magic and fostering literacy, eventually leading to a greater understanding of the "other" aspects of existence.

09
AETTIR

The Aettir are the "families" of runes into which Ancient Futhark is divided. The precise origins of this organization remain uncertain, and numerous artifacts containing inscriptions from the entire Ancient Futhark depict the runes arranged in a single horizontal row instead of the traditional three rows of eight. However, other inscriptions exist that show the runes divided in this way. This can be a useful method for accelerating learning, both historically and in contemporary times. Each Aettir, or family, is named after a deity associated with the initial rune in that particular row. For example, in the first row, the symbol of Fehu represents the Aett of Freyr or the Aett of Frey. The second row presents the symbol of Hagalaz, resulting in the Aett of Heimdall (also known as the Aett of Hagal). Finally, the third row, beginning with the symbol Tiwaz, is called the Aett of Tyr. These divisions facilitate the process of learning and memorizing the various runic forms, while also establishing patterns of interrelationships among the runes that can be used for magical purposes. One approach involves examining the connections between the second runes within each series, namely Uruz, Nauthiz and Berkana, and exploring their respective meanings. Uruz represents brute force, while Nauthiz embodies intense need. Berkana, on the other hand, means birth, encompassing both literal childbirth and, symbolically, the emergence of something new. However, this combination can also denote the need to give birth to a new idea that lends significant force to an undertaking or project. Consequently, these runic relations, together with the specific circumstances of the individual interpreting them, improve the accuracy of their interpretation.

AETT OF FREYR - THE MOTHER

Freyr is the first group or family that symbolizes fertility, which is why it is also called Mother. It is important in giving life and also in how it manifests in our bodies. It is also about awakening our sense of right and wrong. As the first group, Freyr shows us the actions we need to take to achieve our best future. This means we should listen to it and follow it to achieve our greatest goal.

AETT OF HEIMDALL - THE WARRIOR

The god Heimdall leads this second division. He is considered the deity associated with silence, a quality that is also interpreted as pertaining to priestly contemplation. However, in his essence, Heimdall embodies the characteristics of a warrior. He is a vigilant and resolute warrior, adept at facing challenges and difficulties. It is through his unwavering vigilance that he displays unfathomable courage.

AETT OF TYR - THE KING

This group, which can also be seen as the King, represents how people are connected to powerful and magical forces. They also know how they can shape their own futures. This group represents how people act and feel. It shows how people interact with others and how they can change and grow in their hearts and minds.

THE AETT OF FREYR

FEHU ᚠ : CATTLE

Fehu is the first rune of the Elder Futhark. It symbolizes material wealth and prosperity, an earned income, opulence of fortune and future prosperity, both financial and social. When read in reverse, it can represent potential loss, both personal and financial.

URUZ ᚢ : "OX"

Uruz represents a wild bull, a symbol of perseverance and motivation. It reveals vitality, courage, well-being, endurance, quickness, power and masculinity. If reversed, it may suggest a decline in physical or mental strength, or submission to outside influences.

THURISAZ Þ : "MALLET/GIANT"

This rune represents a massive hammer, potentially associated with Thor, or an entity, a giant. It reveals powerful energy, adversity and fortification. In addition, it may symbolize a cleansing or purification process. When reversed, it signifies danger, conflict, devastation and betrayal. Thus, it denotes protection and a mighty surge of energy and strength to counter adversity and conflict.

ANSUZ F : "MESSAGE"

Symbolizes a form of incoming communication, message or insight and can be interpreted as a profound revelation, valuable advice and motivating influence. Conversely, if reversed, it can signify deception or misinterpretation.

RAIDHO R : "JOURNEY"

Raidho is a symbolic representation of a wheel that is on a means of transportation, such as a wagon. It means movement or journey, both physical and spiritual. It conveys notions of advancement, development and expanded viewpoints. When depicted in reverse, it can imply discontinuity or lack of justice.

KENAZ < : "TORCH"

This rune symbolizes a flame or flashlight. The illumination it provides reveals hidden truths, confidential information and even profound insights, such as one's authentic purpose or a surge of inspiration. It serves as a reliable source of guidance. Conversely, when reversed, it exposes obstacles, unpredictability and lack of understanding.

GEBO X : "GIFT"

This rune represents the concept of receiving gifts. It signifies acts of generosity, blessings, demonstration of talent and the creation of harmonious relationships. It is very positive; in fact, there is no reverse interpretation with negative connotations associated with this rune, emphasizing its inherently favorable nature.

WUNJO ᚹ : "JOY"

The rune Wunjo signifies success, achievement, jubilation, harmony and moments of happiness. Conversely, it can also denote suffering and mourning.

THE AETT OF HAGAL OR HEIMDALL

The second Aett of Ancient Futhark is commonly referred to as the Aett of Heimdall or Aett of Hagal. This particular Aett is closely related to the unpredictable and messy aspects of existence. Because of Hagalaz's limited knowledge, he is often associated with Heimdall, the watchful deity who protects Asgard. He diligently protects his realm from any harmful influence, which is promptly signaled by the sound of his horn.

HAGALAZ H : "HAIL"

Also known as Hagalas, Hagal, Hagl, Haal
Sounds like "Ha-ga-lahz."
Sound of the letter: H
Literal translation: hail

Hagalaz is a rune that symbolizes various negative aspects such as hail, destruction, interruption, chaos and misfortune. Hail, in particular, represents the powerful and destructive force of nature. It can appear unexpectedly and cause damage before dissipating. Similar to the inability to control natural phenomena, circumstances beyond our control, such as a severe hailstorm, disease or unforeseen chaos, can inflict damage on us. In turn, this rune may suggest that our progress is hindered, whether in our professional endeavors, personal creative projects, spiritual growth or any other aspect of life. When accompanied by positive surrounding runes, it implies that the obstacle we face is a small one and will not have a significant impact on our overall life trajectory. Conversely, if the surrounding runes are unfavorable, it indicates that the obstacles are major and are likely to persist for a long time. However, it is crucial to remember that hail is temporary. Eventually, the ice shards will melt, leaving behind simple puddles that will evaporate under the heat of the sun.

NAUTHIZ + : "NEEDS"

Also known as Nauth, Nod, Nied, Nautiz, Naudirz.

Sounds like "NAW-theez
Sound of the letter: N
Literal translation: need

Nauthiz means need, scarcity, absence and restriction. Nauthiz is the rune that represents the essential needs of individuals. The symbol of this rune originates from a ceremonial fire that was lit by two large pieces of wood during times of calamity for the ancient Norse, indicating that their needs were being compromised. This rune can imply a lack of satisfaction in one's physical needs, such as hunger, unemployment, or poor health. It can also suggest a lack of mental well-being, potentially leading to isolation, or lack of emotional support, which hinders personal progress. Although correcting these challenges may initially seem insurmountable, it can eventually foster personal growth and enlightenment. Overcoming obstacles can be arduous, but in hindsight one can reflect on their triumphs. Prepared with the wisdom gained from past experiences, future difficulties can be dealt with more effectively. Such challenges are indispensable for personal development. This rune can indicate the need for patience until the time is right to move forward. Alternatively, it serves as a cautionary reminder to avoid succumbing to the destructive behaviors associated with greed. Fixating excessively on one's desires can compromise one's morals and integrity. It is advisable to detach oneself from materialistic activities. Prioritizing essential needs and ignoring ego is essential to focus on what really matters in life.

ISA | : "ICE"

Also known as Eis, Iss, Isaz, Is, Isarz
Sounds like "EE-sah"
Letter sound: I (as in ice)
Literal translation: ice

Isa is a rune that symbolizes ice, freezing, obstacles, delay and stagnation. It represents a state of immobility, both physical and mental. You may have recently experienced exhaustion, hindering your ability to pursue your goals. Perhaps you are facing a mental block, similar to "writer's block," which prevents you from making mental progress. Despite your desire to move forward, it is advisable to accept the current reality rather than resist it. Use this period to focus on your personal development and prepare for future progress. Remember that the ice will melt sooner or later under the heat of the sun. During this period, engage in meditation to clear your mind and improve concentration. The transparency of the ice may symbolize gaining clarity about a particular situation. Alternatively, it could signify a growing emotional distance between you and someone else. The warmth and affection in your relationship may diminish, necessitating a period of reflection. This "cooling off" phase may serve to repair the relationship, or it may eventually lead to its end.

JERA ᛃ : "HARVEST"

Also known as Jer, Jara, Jeran, Jeraz, Gaar, Ar
Sounds like "yare-ah"
Sound of the letter: y
Literal translation: year

Jera symbolizes the year, thus aspects such as harvest, natural cycle, fertility, growth, reward. The passing of the seasons leads to reaping fruits; in fact, this rune represents growth. Like when you plant the seed in the spring, and with hard work you see it grow until it is finally ready to be harvested. This rune also signifies the idea of reaping rewards. Consequently, as the cycle persists, preparations for the coming winter begin. Many paths are in line with the Wheel of the Year, a pagan representation of the cycle of life, in which each phase has its own meaning and purpose, analogous to the seasons. This rune in divination serves to remind individuals of the virtue of patience. Achieving goals takes time and cannot be accelerated. Just as a seed requires months of diligent cultivation before it blossoms and becomes a plant, perseverance eventually leads to success. Conversely, if you are struggling, this rune can signify that difficult times are coming to an end and a promising future awaits.

EIHWAZ ᛇ : "YEW"

Also known as Eoh, Eihuaz, Aihs, Ihwaz
Sounds like "eye-wahz"

Letter sound: ae (as in eye)
Literal translation: yew tree

The symbolism of Eihwaz includes themes of death, rebirth and transformation. Eihwaz is representative of the yew tree, a plant known for its toxic properties to both humans and animals. Historically it was also used as a poison. Consuming any part of the yew tree, including drinking from a cup made of its wood, can prove fatal. However, the concept of death associated with this rune goes beyond its literal meaning. Death can also signify a profound change or transition, similar to the saying "when a door closes, a gateway opens." This symbolism may relate to the end of a relationship, a career, or even a particular lifestyle. It could indicate the abandonment of old habits in favor of spiritual growth, signifying a rebirth. The placement of the yew tree in the center of Elder Futhark suggests that death does not mark the ultimate end. Its central location implies the potential for continuation beyond death, as the yew tree is considered a symbol of life. Ironically, some chemicals in its bark have been used in medical treatments. Also, it is worth noting that Yggdrasil, the mythical world tree, is commonly believed to be a yew tree. Moreover, the yew tree's extraordinary longevity, spanning thousands of years, testifies to its enduring life force.

PERTHRO ⌐ : "DESTINY"

Also known as Perth, Peorth, Peordh, Perdhro, Perthra, Perthu
Sounds like "per-throw"
Sound of the letter: P
Literal translation: cup of dice

Perthro is probably the most controversial of the runic symbols. It symbolizes a cup, thus game, possibility, fate, mystery, destiny. This stems from discord among scholars regarding its precise connotation. Historically, individuals often used cups as a means of gambling, abandoning their fate to the whims of the universe. Therefore, this rune has a profound meaning when it comes to destiny. Although the logic behind the unfolding of life's events may sometimes elude understanding, there is a purpose within these seemingly random events. Until it is revealed, fate remains an enigma. One of the lessons taught by Perthro related to fate is its multifaceted nature, devoid of simplistic categorization into "good" or "bad" outcomes. Instead, one must contemplate the potential impact of destiny. If cast together with other runes that carry negative implications, it could foretell impending disappointment. In such cases, one is advised to exercise caution by refraining from betting one's resources. Given its inscrutable essence, Perthro may signify the imminent revelation of a hidden secret. This clandestine knowledge could include a well-guarded truth from a loved one or even a profound spiritual insight about to be revealed.

As an individual, it is your duty to remain alert to the signs that manifest and tune in to the spiritual energies that permeate your surroundings. Conversely, it may denote the existence of a jealously guarded secret in your being. This may relate to a past experience that you struggle to let go of. This rune can serve as a reminder that clinging to such secrecy is harmful, prompting you to introspect and discover the answers to whatever affliction is plaguing you from within.

ALGIZ Y : "ELK"

Also known as Elhaz, Eolh, Elgr
Sounds like "AL-geez."
Sound of the letter: Z
Literal translation: Elk

Algiz is the rune associated with the majestic elk, symbolizing defensive qualities and opportunity. It serves as a representation of protection, reflecting the way the elk's sturdy antlers protect it from potential threats. By casting this rune, it means that one is protected from harm. However, it does not imply that one should engage in reckless behavior. Despite the assurance of safety, it is essential to remain vigilant to problems and potential dangers. Allow the Divine to guide you in a way that protects you from any harm. Alternatively, this rune may also suggest a disconnect from your intuition. Intuition plays a key role in ensuring personal safety, even beyond physical circumstances. It allows one to discern when others may exploit or inflict emotional harm. Neglecting one's spiritual aspect makes them susceptible to attack.

SOWILO ᛋ : "SUN"

Also known as Sigel, Sol, Sunna, Sowulu
Sounds like "so-WEE-lo."
Sound of the letter: S
Literal translation: sun

Sowilo is an ancient rune associated with the sun, symbolizing triumph, enlightenment, vitality and achievement. The sun, as a source of nourishment and radiance, has great significance. It is worth noting that darkness can cloud our perception, even in a metaphorical sense. If inner darkness is encountered, this rune suggests that it is essential to embrace the light to defeat the darkness. This is true even when the darkness comes from external sources. In the face of emotional harm inflicted by others, it is essential to maintain focus on the light, as it provides clarity. When you are surrounded by the glow, you get better visibility and a greater ability to perceive your surroundings. The presence of light promotes optimism and enlightenment.

THE AETT OF TYR

The deity Tyr embodies the concepts of safeguarding and achieving victories. It also serves as a representation of universal equity and governance issues. This particular set of runes relates to intellect, spiritual development and nonjudgmental understanding. If during the act of divination one were to acquire most of the runes associated with the Tyr set, this might suggest a propensity for passivity in the pursuit of goals. It is possible that excessive contemplation of actions or lack of decisiveness due to uncertainty about one's desires would hinder progress.

TIR/TEIWAZ

Sound: "t"

The initial rune of Tyr's aett, named after God himself, or at least a variation of his name. It symbolizes triumph and equity, similar to the deity. In addition, it is called the rune of the Creator. Similar to Sowilo, invoking Tir generally indicates the potential for success in an endeavor, but may require personal sacrifice. Whether or not this sacrifice is made will determine the catalyst for one's triumph. This rune also proves effective in dealing with complex legal issues, provided one is right. Just like the beginning of Heimdall's aett, Tyr's aett begins with a loss. However, this loss is a voluntary sacrifice. Unlike the hail sent by the gods, the loss suffered at the beginning of the third aett is within one's control. It is possible to proceed without the suggested sacrifice, but it will prove arduous. However, in order to obtain the benefits associated with the subsequent runes, it is necessary to make this sacrifice – just as Tyr had to sacrifice one of his hands to bind the formidable wolf Fenrir, which was believed to have led to Ragnarok. When encountered in a reading, Tyr reversed, the repercussions include a loss of self-confidence, a decrease in trustworthiness in the eyes of others, and cowardice. In essence, it turns us into a weak individual, both physically and mentally. As mentioned earlier, this rune can help persuade a judge to favor one's side, so it is advisable to engrave its symbol on a small piece of wood. The piece should be compact enough to carry in your pocket and take to court.

BERKANO/BERHANO

Sound: "b"

This rune symbolizes the birch tree and indicates a new beginning, much like the growth of the birch tree from a similar tree or a seed planted in the ground. Berkano represents fertility and the creation of a peaceful and harmonious home. If you want to expand your family, you can seek the favor of this rune. In addition, it is effective for maintaining secrecy and confidentiality. If you wish to safeguard something private, the power of Berkano can be beneficial because it ensures that no one reveals your secret. Berkano is mainly about femininity, evident in its resemblance to a pair of breasts. It is a nurturing rune that promotes both physical and spiritual healing. However, when put in a negative light, Berkano can lead to secrecy within all family members, immaturity and a focus on lust rather than fertility. At worst, an inverted Berkano can mean abandonment. To use this rune, it can be engraved on the headboard of the bed of a couple trying to conceive, or placed in stables where animals are expected to give birth.

EHWAZ

Sound: "e"

Ehwaz embodies the divine figures known as Alcis, depicting two brothers on horseback and connected by a wooden beam. This representation serves as a powerful symbol of the inseparable partnership between these twin brothers, and teaches that the actions of one cannot take place without the involvement of the other. In Norse culture, the Ehwaz rune has instructive significance in that the figure of the horse represents the concept of cooperation. Consequently, it relates to all aspects of partnerships, including marriage, relationships and business transactions. Incorporating references to this rune into one's life and connections can strengthen the bonds between partners. Casting the Ehwaz rune also signifies the beginning of a new journey. For example, it could indicate an impending job change or the need to relocate due to professional obligations. Similar to the Tir rune, Ehwaz denotes the beginning of a new beginning, even if it potentially requires sacrifices in return. Another interpretation is the importance of following the natural course of a task at hand, emphasizing the importance of harmonious cooperation with others rather than constant conflict. It also suggests the need to rely on and cooperate with others to successfully complete all efforts. In contrast, the inverted position of this rune indicates some negative implications, such as betrayal and impulsive haste in carrying out tasks, which often lead to unfavorable results. It may also foreshadow the collapse of stable relationships. In Neopagan unions, partners often adorn their hands with the painted Ehwaz rune as a symbol of their eternal union, serving as a testimony to their mutual trust and loyalty.

MANNAZ

Sound: "m"

The rune known as Mannaz has great significance as it symbolizes humanity. It has the power to represent one's ethnicity or individuality. This rune possesses unique qualities that can be applied in various social contexts and purposes. It also helps strengthen bonds among group members and promotes a rational mindset when dealing with disagreements. By casting Mannaz, one embarks on a journey of self-analysis and inner contemplation. When faced with a challenging task and seeking guidance, casting this rune can provide the answers sought. In addition, Mannaz can serve as a reminder to focus on personal reputation and interpersonal skills. Rather than blaming others within a group, choosing Mannaz when facing difficulties in collaboration signals a desire to improve oneself. Conversely, it can also signify a strong and capable team that thrives on unity. However, in negative cases, Mannaz warns of minor problems that escalate and negatively affect collaboration. It can also indicate unintentional sabotage and a gradual weakening of ties. To promote family serenity, it is advisable to inscribe this symbol on the table, as it amplifies the shared bond within the family and promotes productive conversations.

LAGUZ

Sound: "l"

This rune symbolizes the water element and its fluid characteristics, representing the power and adaptability of water as it flows. Laguz indicates the importance of human thought in promoting positive results. When Laguz appears in a rune reading, it can be interpreted as a place of refuge from the negativity of the world. It can symbolize a supportive partner or a harmonious relationship that can be relied upon in difficult times. Drawing Laguz also signifies the wise decision to trust your intuition in handling the tasks at hand. By following your intuition, you allow yourself to be guided to the correct path without overthinking and creating unnecessary obstacles. Laguz highlights the occasional need to let the unconscious mind take the lead, as it could offer valuable insights. However, an inverted Laguz position suggests the possibility of emotional manipulation by someone close to you. Engraving Laguz on an amulet or similar object can improve your mental abilities and promote further learning. In addition, the Laguz effect can strengthen your intuition, enabling you to make better decisions.

INGUZ/ING

Sound: "ng"

Inguz is a rune concerning sexuality, as it holds dominion over physical attraction to others and, ultimately, sexual activity. Its influence mainly concerns reproduction and fertility. The use of Inguz also grants the ability to distribute one's energy at will, thus enabling one to impact more individuals or provide protection to an important group. However, it is essential to build up energy gradually in order to effectively harness the power of Inguz. Once you reach a certain threshold, you can release this energy all at once, or gradually. Encountering Inguz in a reading can also signify the need to use good judgment in decision making, particularly if we tend to blindly follow the actions of those around us without considering the potential consequences. The presence of this rune can serve as a reminder to stop and use good judgment to recognize if you are on an unfavorable path. If an inverted Inguz rune appears, there is generally no cause for concern, as it often represents minor inconveniences such as lust or immaturity. However, it could also indicate decreased libido or fertility. In addition to rune casting, Inguz can be used in various other ways. For example, one can engrave the symbol on a small piece of wood and carry it in one's pocket to increase the chances of attracting a partner. Also, carving this rune on the headboard of the bed can enhance one's sexual experiences.

DAGAZ

Sound: "d"

Dagaz, also recognized as the "Rune of Transformation," embodies profound metamorphosis encompassing spiritual, mental and social aspects. Commonly called the Rune of Dawn, it symbolizes the significant transition from night to day, which is undeniably immense. If you seek guidance in making critical decisions, Dagaz is among the runes that can offer assistance. Its appearance also indicates the need to reassess current circumstances and contemplate whether drastic change is necessary. It means judging the correctness of your decisions. During a reading session, Dagaz can also convey the concept of balance between opposing forces, such as light and darkness, serving as a cue to identify the need for adjustments to achieve balance in your life. The distinctive attribute of this rune is the rare presence of reverse effects. However, when surrounded by opposite and reversed runes, it can imply the imperative to look forward and refrain from dwelling excessively on the past. Given Dagaz's association with transformation, it would be appropriate to inscribe it on the doors of schools or any other institution of learning. Moreover, it would be especially relevant in rehabilitation centers, as those undergoing hospitalization aspire to undergo a positive metamorphosis.

OTHALA/OTHILA

Sound: "o"

Othala is the rune that symbolizes loyalty, particularly loyalty to family, clan, tribe, country or creed. Similar to Fehu, Othala represents wealth, but differs in that its wealth is not materialistic. Rather, it encompasses the values of family, culture, heritage and friendships. Othala signifies a sense of restraint and balance. Its presence in a reading often indicates issues related to ancestral birthrights. For example, there may be important information or connections in your town that would be worth exploring. This rune may also indicate significant developments involving close relatives, such as a desire for reconciliation after a long period of estrangement. In addition, it could suggest a call from your country or culture to contribute your skills, such as enlisting in the military. It could also mean that it is advisable to safeguard your assets in the near future. It is important to note that the misuse of this rune can lead to the harmful development of racism, bigotry and xenophobia. Unfortunately, during World War II, Othala was engraved on the knives of Hitler Youth members, exemplifying its misuse. If you seek to harness the energy of this rune, it is advisable to do so in conjunction with something associated with family matters.

ODIN'S RUNE

In contemporary usage, the optional white rune, commonly called Odin's Rune, can be incorporated into divination rune sets. Its presence indicates our incomplete understanding, but recognizes this lack of knowledge as acceptable. Central to Norse belief is the Wyrd principle, which recognizes the interconnectedness of all things in the universe. It emphasizes that one's actions, or lack thereof, have the potential to impact not only one's own life but also the lives of others, regardless of their physical proximity. Reflecting the essence of the Wyrd, respect for nature is inherent in Norse paganism. Practitioners are environmentally conscious and understand that the Earth must be cared for and cultivated to maintain its abundance. In modern neopaganism and pagan practices, an additional empty rune called Wyrd, meaning destiny, has been introduced along with the traditional 24 runes of the Futhark runic alphabet. This rune embodies both the concept of total emptiness and infinite possibilities, depending on one's perspective. The Odin rune, a later addition of the Neopagans, is used by rune readers to tap into cosmic forces for better divination. Its appearance indicates the presence of the unknown, even if it remains invisible. Despite its widespread use, the precise meaning of the Odin rune has always been debated, with some interpreting it as a representation of infinite possibilities while others perceive it as a symbol of emptiness. The meaning of this rune can be compared to the ancient philosophical question of whether a glass is half full or half empty.

WHAT IS MEANT BY AN EMPTY RUNE

When you encounter an empty rune, it is important to consider that it may indicate complications in the casting process. It might suggest that your request is not being formulated correctly or that the answer you seek is elusive (or perhaps, after all, you already have the answer). Take it as a signal to engage in meditation and exercise patience before attempting another reading. The consensus on Odin's rune is nonexistent. Ask for the opinions of ten people and you will receive ten different answers. The white rune does not possess an unambiguous definition. Any potential user can use it at his or her own discretion. In his publication "A Manual for the Use of an Ancient Oracle" (1983), Ralph Blum postulates that the appearance of the white rune foretells an omen of death. However, this death is purely symbolic and does not represent the actual death of an individual. It can also signify the beginning of a particular aspect of life and its replacement by another. Lisa Peschel, author of "A Practical Guide to Runes: Their Uses in Divination and Magic," says that whenever this rune emerges, one can only anticipate the occurrence of something unexpected. This event can be positive or negative, depending on one's virtuosity. It is also advisable to interpret its meaning in relation to adjacent runes. Kylie Holmes, author of "Pagan Portals: Runes" (2013), suggests that casting the empty rune signifies progress in one's spiritual development. This act also serves as a reminder of the vastness of one's knowledge. Throughout its existence of more than a millennium, the runic alphabet has undergone minimal alterations. Variations typically occur geographically, with only slight changes to the shape of some runes. However, their meaning has remained unchanged. However, a modern addition to the Elder and Younger Futhark runic alphabets is the Wyrd rune. Concrete evidence for the existence of the Wyrd rune (also known as Odin's rune) prior to the revival of rune use is lacking, and its origins are puzzling to say the least. However, it is now included in most rune sets.

WHY THE WYRD RUNE IS CONSIDERED DIFFERENT

The Wyrd rune is often just an empty tile in the set, but some claim that: "This runic symbol represents all forms of runes fashioned into one."

According to ancient beliefs, it is possible to personally create this rune using clay or a similar substance. Regardless of the material chosen, it would be imperative to acquire a small amount of material from the other runes to create a new one. The white rune serves as the culmination of the powers possessed by all the other runes. Differing from the three Aettir of Ancient Futhark, the white rune stands apart from the others. It is a relatively recent addition, emerging about four decades ago, in the 1980s, during the rise of the New

Age movement in Western society. However, despite its recent inclusion in the runic alphabet, the white rune is still widely adopted by contemporary runic engravers. Moreover, the white rune differs from the rest of the runic alphabet in that it originates primarily from an ancient script. Consequently, with the exception of the Wyrd, each rune represents a specific sound or combination of sounds. Some practitioners claim that the Wyrd symbolizes silence, presenting a distinctive concept since no other alphabet in the world presents a symbol of silence. Traditional beliefs also suggest that empty runes existed exclusively as replacement tiles in case another tile was lost or misplaced. Purists argue that the white rune does not align with the mathematical and mystical system of runes. This is due to the impossibility of dividing twenty-five tiles equally into four, representing the four seasons of the year, the four cardinal directions and other aspects. The Wyrd rune does not have its own set of definitions. It can also be interpreted as complete emptiness or unlimited possibilities. In addition, some perceive it as a symbol of hidden forces operating behind the scenes to influence one's destiny.

WHY IT IS ALSO CALLED ODIN'S RUNE

The Wyrd rune is also known as the Odin rune because of its deep and enigmatic power and meaning. Odin, the Supreme Being and ruler of the gods of Asgard, is constantly seeking knowledge. The association between the white rune and Odin is due not only to his omnipotence, but also to his insatiable thirst for knowledge. When Odin is present in a reading, he urges introspection to reach a deeper understanding of oneself and existence. The empty rune symbolizes the unlimited potential of humanity, and it is up to the interpreter to determine how to harness this knowledge. This is also why Odin's rune is not part of the Aettir, as Odin is isolated, distinct from the other Aesir gods. Trying to attach further meaning to Odin's rune is like trying to connect all the Nine Worlds with a thread: it would be futile and impossible.

HOW TO READ AN EMPTY RUNE

Although not all rune experts agree on the inclusion of the empty rune in all sets, there is no prohibition against its use if you wish. If you want to incorporate the Odin rune into your readings, here are some suggestions on how to interpret it. One approach to deciphering the meaning of the white rune is to rely on the concept of Orlog. The ancient Anglo-Saxons, along with various other tribal societies in what is now Northern Europe, firmly believed in the omnipresent force known as Orlog, which meant "destiny." Orlog governs the destiny of all nations and their inhabitants. Norns were deities in Norse mythology, and the term means to whisper (a secret). This suggests that the Norns grant you an individual destiny if you encounter this rune. Therefore, the white rune can be seen as a messenger of news. Extracting it in a reading could indicate that you have a karmic debt and that the cosmos is collecting payment. Therefore, encountering this rune may mean that you need to do better in your current and future life. Another plausible interpretation of the empty rune is that you have reached a point of no return in life's journey. You are inevitably headed toward a definite destiny and are doing nothing to change it. Although you still have a choice, if you continue on the same path, the results will always be the same. However, encountering the empty rune in response to a specific question means that it is not the right time for your request. Fate may still have something in store for the next part of your life, so it is not yet present in the rune reading. Another explanation that can be derived from the empty rune is that you will experience great changes. Obviously, because of the ambiguous nature of this rune, you cannot be sure whether the change will be negative or positive.

IS IT RECOMMENDED TO USE THE WYRD RUNE?

The decision to include the empty rune in your rune set is entirely up to you. Traditionalists may deride its use, considering it a deviation from Ancient Futhark. Some even consider it sacrilegious. It is important to note that not everyone accepts the empty rune, particularly those who adhere strictly to traditional beliefs. They see it as a modern invention born out of a desire for new age spirituality and disdain for sacred symbols. To them, a rune should represent something, not nothingness. Despite these criticisms, the concept of the empty rune has gained ground over the past four decades within neopaganism. It has undergone constant scrutiny and rejection by the rune community, leading some producers to explicitly state whether or not they include it in their sets. It is worth mentioning that the original set of 24 runes did not contain the empty rune; it was not introduced until the 1980s. The question of whether it is appropriate to use the empty rune remains open, so the decision is solely an individual preference. If one is looking for a more authentic and traditional runic reading, it may be better to forgo the empty rune. However, for those who are open to experimentation and aligned with the beliefs of the neopagan New Age movement, there is no harm in incorporating the empty rune into their practice. My advice is to try it during self-readings to determine if it fits with your personal style. Armed with knowledge of the origins and use of the empty rune, individuals can form their own opinions about its inclusion. Regardless of personal choice, it is undeniable that the hollow rune has made its mark in the world of traditional runic reading and may continue to do so for a long time.

10
RUNES TIPS AND SECRETS

CREATING A SET OF RUNES

The bonds we form with friends and family are based on respect and affection, and lead to deep and lasting relationships. Likewise, runes can be seen as trusted allies and deserve to be treated with respect. Cultivating a positive partnership with this divinatory tool is always beneficial, as it has the power to improve our lives. When creating a personal set of runes, it is essential to approach the task with care and dedication. It is advised never to give or lend one's runes to others, as these creations are intended solely for the owner. Transferring ownership would imply breaking the personal bond. When individuals fashion their own runic symbols, they imbue them with their own energy and strength, infusing a part of themselves into these objects. The purpose of runic creations is solely to serve the interests and goals of the creator. Although it is possible to temporarily share these objects, most practitioners prefer to keep their runic sets reserved for their own religious, magical and divinatory purposes. Occasionally, acquaintances or even strangers may request a personal reading. In such circumstances, outside influences may be encountered. Some people have trouble maintaining boundaries, which can strain relationships. They may become annoying and express illogical opinions. It is perfectly acceptable to ignore these individuals and continue on one's way. Not everyone understands the significance of the small piece of wood or other material that has been infused with their own energy and life force. To some, the Norse religion, and all that comes with it, may seem like pure folklore or even fanaticism. We should not be discouraged and fear the judgment of others, but pursue our own beliefs and future plans. As mentioned above, runic symbols can be made from various natural materials, such as pebbles, wood, stone or clay. The choice of material depends on personal preference. Symbols on runes can be painted in various colors on both wooden and clay surfaces. Their purpose is to fulfill our needs and desires. It is essential to handle them with the utmost care and consideration. Although runes can be drawn on any natural material, wood is the most commonly used. Wooden runes possess a special charm, although they do not last long. Few ancient runes have survived to shed light on their origins. Among the oldest known examples of ancient Norse runes are STAFR (representing a pentagram, letter, or secret), TEINN (a twig symbolizing divination), and HLUTR (a divinatory instrument or object). In some Germanic tribes, fruit wood was used to inscribe runic symbols, as evidenced by the writings of the famous Latin writer Tacitus. However, other sources suggest that runic symbols were actually carved into ash wood. Both accounts may contain some truth. The material used is less significant than the personal significance of the rune to the individual. It is advisable to make a meaningful connection with the material chosen in order to feel a closer connection with divine energy. The rune set would be more fulfilling if the material used had a personal touch. The decision regarding the material for inscribing runic symbols can be influenced by various factors. Some select a specific tree for its herbal, medicinal, or magical properties, while others choose a tree based on childhood memories associated with it. Once the appropriate material has been chosen, it is necessary to determine the appropriate shape and size for the runes. It is essential to ensure that all 25 tiles can fit comfortably in people's palms. Ideally the measurements should be around 4 cm in length, a width of 3 cm or less, and a maximum thickness of about 1 cm. When it comes to shape, round runes are the easiest to carve. If wood is your favorite material, collect it in the wild, taking only what you really need. Be sincere in your intentions. Some individuals even offer coins as a form of payment to the tree, burying them under its roots. Since trees are living things, it is important to ask their permission before breaking a branch and express gratitude for their contribution. Once you have obtained a piece of wood from your favorite tree, cut it into 25 equal pieces of the same size. Removal of the bark is not mandatory. Those who prefer not to cut off a tree branch can easily obtain dowels at a nearby lumber mill. Although the choice may be less personal, it is possible to find dowels made of the desired wood, such as pine, oak or ash. Carving and drawing runic symbols on wood can be achieved with a sharp tool and using markers or paint. Although carving and painting require significant effort, they are often preferred because doing it personally contributes to a more mystical experience. Some people possess a natural talent for painting, while others may find themselves hesitant in front of a paintbrush. Beginners are advised to use acrylic paints, which allow for easy application and the creation of intricate runic designs. Alternatively, markers are an easy option for those unfamiliar with brushes and paints. Indelible markers glide smoothly over wood surfaces, are available in a wide range of colors, and do not fade easily. For best results, it is recommended to select a lighter shade tint than the wood you choose. However, tints have some drawbacks, such as discoloration, which causes the desired effect to be lost. Colors effectively seal the pores of the material, but this also results in the loss of the wood's natural texture. Applying a clear liquid sealant is also expected, as it gives a lot of shine, but it can make the runes appear artificial and lacking in their inherent energies. One tip is to avoid any marks on the back of the created runes. The presence of such markings could lead to distortions in the selection process. Ensuring the absence of identifying marks can guarantee unbiased selection when the runes are turned face down. For these reasons, it is essential to refrain from decorating or leaving any kind of identifying mark on the back. If the runes are circular in shape, it may be helpful to mark a simple line on the back to indicate their north-south axis. Before undertaking the creation of the runes, try to grasp their meaning. Focus your attention and recognize that you are performing an important task, bringing an ancient tradition back to life, and that through this process you will gain greater control over your life, environment and world. Express gratitude and recognize the deep meaning behind the creation of these divine tools. You are not simply shaping material, but making connections with entities that will offer you spiritual guidance throughout your life. Before carving the runes, take a moment to meditate and offer prayers to the deities. This seemingly simple act can elevate your material crafting project to the status of a sacred ritual. Runes can be used by individuals of any religious background, whether Christian or pagan, monotheist or polytheist. It is important, however, to fully acknowledge and accept the runic system and beliefs of the Norse people with respect and humility. Personal beliefs regarding religion should not interfere with or disturb the way these gods and forces have permeated the lives of the followers of the runic system. To truly understand and enhance the power and effectiveness of runic symbols, a comprehensive understanding of the Norse people, their unique deities and the significant role of runes within their community is essential. Only through a genuine and deep understanding, which goes beyond mere knowledge of the runic system, can one immerse oneself in the atmosphere of the ancient runic tradition. Maximum benefits can be derived from this process. Odin and Freya were the guardians of the runes, and many followers worship them for help and wisdom. If we make a comparison with other religions, we can compare Odin to Jehovah, since this is his role in the Norse pantheon. To understand the figure of Freya, we can imagine her as the beginning of growth, development and light, divinely represented by the arrival of spring. Those who practice the use of runes hold the connection with these two deities in high regard because it is seen as a means of personal growth and spiritual advancement. Ancient runic symbols not only possess the power to effect magical and divinatory changes, but also played a significant role in the transition from paganism to Christianity. Contrary to popular belief, this transformation was not a rapid process, particularly for the lower classes who saw no immediate benefits in abandoning their old beliefs. It was the ruling and upper classes who were the first to embrace the new faith, motivated by political and social benefits. However, the majority of society, consisting of the poorer class, remained steadfast in their traditional religious beliefs. Surprisingly, Iceland remained faithful to its ancient faith the longest, maintaining its pagan culture until the 11th century. Even today, Iceland remains a vibrant center for those interested in experiencing and learning about Norse traditions. When creating your runes, it is possible that you may harbor anxiety toward working with the materials, perhaps due to unfamiliarity with the tools or fear of ruining your creations with inadequate painting skills. However, do not allow uncertainties to consume you and stop you. Just like any artist beginning the creation of his or her first works, pick up your tools and create your runes. Should wood prove daunting, consider using stone as a wonderful alternative. Renowned in jewelry craftsmanship, it is a very versatile material that is readily available on the market. Engraving it is a simple task, requiring nothing more than judicious application of creativity and imagination. In addition, small metal discs, readily available in markets and fairs, can be made into pendants. Their ease of engraving and painting allows for the rectification of any unsightly previous work, giving you the opportunity to correct your mistakes. Apply yourself completely and with dedication, and rest assured that the fruits of your labor will be nothing short of extraordinary. I can guarantee that it will be worth it.

SUITABLE MATERIALS

• STONE RUNES

The most suitable stones for creating runes are those that possess a smooth texture and are flexible enough to be easily carved, particularly those found in riverbeds. To begin the process, it is imperative to locate small stones of relatively uniform size. Next, these stones can be customized to individual preferences by selecting a color that is suitable and enhances the connection with the runes. Once the desired color has been chosen, it is recommended that the resulting stones be meticulously painted. To ensure their durability, a protective coating should be applied or an alternative sealing method should be used.

• RUNES WITH WOOD

If you do not reside near a river or lake where smooth stones are readily available, you should use an alternative material. Wood proves to be an excellent choice in such circumstances because of its malleability and ability to transform easily. For the creation of runes, it is most advantageous to use wood with a round shape, typically in the shape of a disc. Fallen branches are an optimal source for creating excellent runes. Unlike stones, where it is necessary to paint the Rune marks, wood allows for greater flexibility. This makes it possible to engrave the symbols and later use paint or markers for decoration to enhance their visual appeal. The technique used to affix the symbol to the rune will influence the final coloring. In addition, natural wood can be used for the runes, eliminating the need to color it.

• RUNES WITH CLAY

Clay is a material that possesses a high degree of flexibility and malleability, facilitating the work of creation. It allows the desired runic forms to be shaped, effortlessly. After the molding process, it becomes imperative to engrave the runic symbols on the surface. To ensure their durability, the runes must be fired in a kiln. In addition, clay offers more creative possibilities, allowing the application of different techniques to embellish and decorate them.

- ## RUNES MADE FROM BONES

Using animal bones to create runes is a sensible practice, although it requires a good deal of skill. The complexities of bone material make it inherently difficult to manipulate and shape into the desired runic forms. Therefore, a certain level of experience and manual dexterity in this field is essential to successfully carve bone and create runes. Without such skills, the runes run the risk of being subject to frequent chipping and irreparable damage. If you lack experience and manual dexterity with this material, use those mentioned above, which are simpler and easier.

CHOOSING COLORS

After obtaining twenty-five matching pieces, it is time to adorn the runic system symbols with paint. The choice of color is entirely up to one's discretion, allowing a personalized touch to each rune. Deliberating on material and color selection fosters a deeper connection with these ancient symbols. In case of color confusion, one can always opt for the usual shades. The traditional palette offers a range of colors capable of exerting a mystical influence on both the runes and the subconscious of their possessor. Red is the most frequently used traditional color in runic magic, as it represents the active male principle and life force embodied in the color of blood. Blue also finds widespread use in runes, symbolizing Odin and commonly used by practitioners imploring his blessings. In addition, blue signifies healing, making it a favorable choice. Green, on the other hand, embodies prosperity, fertility and growth, particularly favored by sorceresses. However, there is no obligation to select any of the traditional colors. One should follow one's intuition when it comes to one's personal set of runes, painting them in the colors that resonate most with one's individual preferences.

CONTAINERS FOR RUNES

To ensure the preservation of one's runes, it is advisable to store them in a special case. This not only keeps all the runes organized and protected in one place, but also simplifies the process of transporting them from one place to another. The case should be the size to hold all twenty-five runes. It is advisable to own a case made of natural materials. Options available, for followers who use runes, include fur, linen, and cotton. The case can range from a simple cotton bag to a finely decorated wallet; the choice is subjective. Some devote time and effort to embellishing their pouch, while others prefer a more minimalist approach. You can create a simple leather case by making vertical slits in the top to pass a strap or drawstring through and tighten it. When constructing a fabric bag, it is important to leave an extra inch at the top and sew as close to the edge as possible, ensuring ample room for buttonholes. Opting for red is considered an excellent choice, as it is reputed to be an auspicious color. It exudes positive, vibrant and mystical energies. Moreover, it is crucial to remember that one's choices should not be dictated solely by tradition. Instead, it is intuition that should guide these decisions, just as in the choice of material to create runic symbols. Therefore, use your intuition; you will surely not go wrong. In addition, you can adorn your container with embroidered symbols, tassels, bells or any object that has a special and deep meaning for you.

THE READING CLOTH

The rune cloth is a simple white cloth specially designed for casting runes. The color white is highly recommended because of its association with purity and truth. Neutrality is essential for a runic cloth, so it must be free of any distractions such as prints or designs. No elaborate decorations or designs are necessary, as the main goal is to prevent the mind and eye from being distracted. One must focus exclusively on the runes. Although the fabric can also be different colors (light shades), simplicity and clarity are essential and necessary elements. The material used need not be extraordinary; any basic fabric, soft or hard, old or new, will suffice. The main purpose of the fabric is to maintain the cleanliness of the runes. To infuse the runes with your own energy, it is advisable to keep them closed as much as possible in the chosen container. Your personal vibrations will leave an indelible imprint, making them more personalized. The rune case can be worn on your belt, carried in your purse, or even held on your legs while doing activities such as reading or watching TV. It is recommended to place it on the solar plexus region, which is located between the diaphragm and the navel. This specific location is critical because it corresponds to the energy center of the human body and where the person's aura is most strongly felt. Alternatively, you can place the bag under the pillow before sleeping. This approach during sleep has obvious advantages as it often leads to meaningful dreams with runic themes. Although it is not necessary for the runes to be in constant contact with you, it is advisable to have them close by for a significant period of time. It is essential to make an effort to tune the runes to one's "wavelength" before embarking on any serious attempt at divination.

11
PRESERVING THE RUNES

If you want your runes to maintain their original efficiency, you must take diligent care of them. Unlike other accessories, maintaining runes goes beyond simple cleaning rituals. It involves both purifying and recharging them. Runes hold great potential as divinatory tools, particularly when handled with the utmost care and reverence. It becomes imperative to cleanse and empower them, especially if they are new or have been handled by numerous people. It is critical to recognize that runes are deeply personal and private property, reserved exclusively for the use and safekeeping of their owners. You may choose to place them on your workspace or desk, or perhaps even keep them near your bed. By maintaining such proximity, you allow the runes to attune to your personal energy, thus facilitating clearer and more authentic divinations.

CLEANSING THE RUNES

There are many ways to clean the runes. You can choose the one you like best, but the important thing is to do it often and regularly. Cleaning becomes even more important between uses or when they are surrounded by other people's energy for too long. Here's how to clean the runes so they work properly again:

- Store them outside the house in the evening or early morning for at least 24 hours.

- *Smudging* - This method involves passing smoke from the burning of certain herbs, which have properties primarily intended to purify them. Sage is the most commonly used herb, but other herbs such as cedar, lavender and myrrh are also used. If you live in an area where even a small fire can cause panic among neighbors, you can replace the herbs with a white candle.

- You can also clean them using natural running water, such as from a stream near you. Never use tap water, as it has undergone multiple treatment processes to make it drinkable. If you have rainwater stored in a container at home, you can use it.

CONSECRATING THE RUNES

By continuously using the runes, you will gradually learn about the forces of nature. You will understand your place in the universe and experience growth in all aspects. Nature teaches us how to maintain balance and harmony. When you regularly interact with nature and its constituent elements, you cannot help but feel enlightened and empowered. If you do this regularly, you will increasingly grow your connection with the universe. In addition to communicating with nature, you can also empower yourself by wearing runic symbols. Runes emit powerful vibrations and serve as protection from evil. They will attract the positive qualities of life. By wearing a rune around your neck as a talisman, your whole being will be affected by the rune and its influence. If you have just purchased or created a new rune set, or have been using it for a while, you should consecrate it before using it again. Not only will it give you new energy, but your readings will be more uniform and accurate. Sanctification means to make something holy. When you sanctify a rune, it is transformed from an ordinary stone or wooden dowel into a sacred tool for divination. The beauty of runes is that they can be reconsecrated indefinitely. If you have recently realized that your readings have become less clear or accurate, you should consecrate them as soon as possible. One thing to remember when you consecrate a rune is that you are not only purifying the rune and preparing it for use, but you are also creating a spiritual bond between the rune and you. This is why you don't have to be psychic to use runes. The runes themselves act as a bridge between you and God. Anyone who can read the runes becomes a divine interpreter, and can get directions from the universe. When you interpret the readings, you will find that they tell a story, and you can use the messages you receive to figure out your next course of action. To access the messages and stories hidden within the runes, it is helpful to consecrate the set of runes. This applies whether you use them for a self-reading or to provide readings to others. Although psychic abilities are not necessary to read the runes, consecration improves your perception and allows you to anticipate answers even before casting the runes. It is advisable to keep track of any thoughts that come to mind during a reading and check later to see if they are in line with the result. Moving on to the actual consecration process, similar to purification, there is no one-size-fits-all method for consecrating runes. Adhering to the basic requirements can be done effectively. The first requirement is the use of purifying smoke. Sage is commonly used by most pagan practitioners for its properties, although some individuals may find its scent unbearable. Traditional incense and myrrh are reliable alternative choices, but a white unscented candle can perform the same task and act as a catalyst, through its warm light. Choose the method that works best for you.

The basic steps for a consecration ceremony are as follows:

- Light the sage/incense beam and allow the smoke to flow over you, purifying yourself and the rune container.

- Hold the runes with your non-dominant hand. Hold it above the sage/incense smoke or the white candle flame. The hand should be high enough not to feel pain.

- Seek the protection of the deities and protect the runes from outsiders except the highest forms of energy.

- Connect with each rune, and imagine your energy entering each one and becoming one. Now, with your non-dominant hand, grasp them all again and place them over the smoke. Ask the deity of your choice to consecrate them so that their use will help you and others. After cleaning and consecrating the set, you can use them right away. When not in use, it is best to store them in a lined box or soft bag so that they remain safe and do not lose their sacredness.

Here is another method for consecrating runes

- Clean the runes thoroughly, go on to anoint the throat and heart and the third eye (located above the root of the nose at a central point on the forehead), with a few drops of sacred oil or water.

- Use a small dose of the same substance by applying it to each rune with your finger. Concentrate on the runes trying to gain their full strength and presence so as to strengthen yourself inwardly.

EMPOWERING THE RUNES

To empower the runes, you can keep them in your pocket or purse, or in your personal space. In this way, they can tune into your personal energy. Here are some other suggestions:

- Leave the runes outside at first light and bring them back inside before sunset.

- Bury the set of runes in the ground; they will incorporate the energy of the earth.

Put them inside a bag, make a hole in the ground and bury them. You can dig them up after at least a week.

- You can also perform purification ceremonies, here's how to do it. First, form a circle to expel any negative energy, then clear the space and use smoke from a pile of sage, or alternative herb, that you set on fire. Lay the throwing cloth in the center of the circle and the runes to be purified. Bless the runes with the main elements of nature. You can choose what has important meaning for you. For example, for the air element, pass them through sage smoke. For the earth element, sprinkle them with coarse salt. Sprinkle them with rainwater for the water element. Finally, for the fire element, pass through the flame of a burning red candle. After completing these rituals, hold each rune firmly in your right hand to imbue it with your soul. It is best to clean them before and after each use if you usually use the runes for a reading to other people.

RECHARGING THE RUNES

It is appropriate to reload the runes before the first reading, but you can choose to reload them as often as you like, whenever you want to give them a "revamp."

To recharge the runes:

- Get comfortable and breathe deeply several times.

- If using crystals (they are optional), arrange them around the runes.

- With your fingers, trace the shape of each rune, speaking its name (or sound) and focusing on its meaning.

- Repeat the process until you feel an aura of magic emanating from the runes. Place them back in the case (which you will need to purify and consecrate), and leave them inside for some time, ready for the next castings.

CREATING A SACRED SPACE

To be successful, you do not need a specific environment to perform the ritual. But a piece of advice for you readers approaching this fascinating world, is to carry out the reading, in a quiet, familiar place filled with positive energy. The use of runes, also requires a receptive and calm mind to truly listen to their wisdom. Creating a sacred space for readings allows one to calm the mind, make meaningful connections and understand that divination is not to be taken lightly. The knowledge gained from the readings must be incorporated into one's daily life, a process that takes time and commitment. Without dedication to the practice, how can one hope to gain true wisdom? It is essential to find a space, both inside and outside, that is free of clutter and conducive to introspection. Consider incorporating elements such as music, incense, candles, essential oils, crystals and plants into your rituals and readings.

Consistency in using the same space and basic elements for most rituals fosters a deeper connection with the mystic. However, small changes can be made to suit the specific reading. Lighting specific candles or selecting different crystals or talismans can enhance the experience depending on the topic at hand. By allowing the spirit to guide you, you will eventually find the ideal balance between repeating the ritual and adapting to the situation.

PREPARING FOR CASTING

Prepare your space before beginning the launch, making sure you have all the necessary items such as candles, a lighter, and a pen. Hydrate and relax to avoid interruptions or distractions. Prepare appropriately for the occasion, such as wearing your favorite dress for matters of love, or pouring a glass of good wine when the reading concerns financial matters.

Tradition calls for an altar physically placed below the seated reader, such as a low table, but there are many options, so look for the best way to be comfortable. Make sure you have ample space and easily accessible writing materials while reading the runes. Arrange talismans, journal, and any other necessary items on the cloth according to personal intuition. Place the bag of runes in the center of the cloth and light candles or incense, or opt for diffusing oils if you prefer. Invoke the spirits you wish to invite to the ceremony. When the environment and vibrations are favorable, you may want to close your eyes and take a few deep breaths. While inhaling, you should be aware that this act helps to release mental, emotional and physical loads. It revitalizes the blood and awakens the mind. This procedure allows distractions, doubts, fears and tensions to be removed. If desired, it is also possible to engage in melodic chanting or vocalization. The vocalization serves to focus the mind in the context of the reading and to respectfully present oneself to the runes within the ritual. Sit down, imagining your feet and spine sinking like tree roots into the earth. Try to synchronize your heartbeat, with that of the earth. Also, you should be aware of the activating presence of the sun and moon on the top of your head. Your palms should be facing upward, indicating readiness to receive. Once a sense of calm and stability is achieved, the casting of the runes can begin.

12
READING THE RUNES

READING TECHNIQUES

Reading runes is a very complex and mystical practice. It can be seen as a quest for prediction or a method of connecting people who seek advice or divinatory intervention. Based on the different categories of runes, there are different categories of alphabet. Ancient Futhark is undeniably the most popular, probably because it has the most letters. However, the commonly used procedure for reading runes is as follows:

Step 1 - Place all the runes in a bag, and mix the contents. Close your eyes and immerse yourself in deep contemplation, directing your attention to a past, present or future situation. Once the revelation materializes, take out the number of runes from the bag, according to the chosen pattern.

Step 2 - Place the runes on the reading cloth as you meditate on the answer you desire for your situation. Next, look at which runes you have extracted.

Step 3 - Arrange the runes following the chosen pattern for reading, close your eyes, concentrate and run your hand over them as you think about the questions you want answers to. If you are left-handed, use your right hand and vice versa. Concentrate and seek inspiration through meditation and spiritual connection. If your mind is focused, you will get your answer.

PATTERNS FOR SELF-READINGS

- If you want to get an immediate and frank answer about your situation, with your eyes closed, pull three runes out of the bag and line them up. Open your eyes and read the answers for your past, present and future situation according to the reading of the extracted runes.

- Another method of reading consists of choosing two runes from the bag. Depending on the meaning given to each of them, the options can be two: they will either complement each other, or oppose each other. If they have the same meaning, for example, they will support you greatly, but if they oppose each other, it means that one thing will happen followed by the other. Instead, by selecting three runes and arranging them side by side, you can discover answers to physical, mental and spiritual conditions, respectively.

To get information about your inner well-being use one of the above patterns.

Reading and interpreting runes is a practice that may seem complicated at first, especially when trying to interpret the meanings attributed to each individual rune. The advice is to study and apply yourself, and everything will become less nebulous and you will acquire more and more skills. Beginners can develop familiarity and understanding through practice. The next few paragraphs will deal with Layots (reading patterns). It is an essential and indispensable concept for becoming infallible rune readers. My advice is.....Apply and experiment!

WRITING WITH RUNES

Although runes have been used as an alphabet since the first century AD, their mystical qualities and associations with divination continue to fascinate people today. A popular application of written runes is the creation of scriptures, in which individuals attempt to compose personal or enigmatic messages that could in some way determine their fate. Runes differ from conventional languages, so the usual rules of writing do not apply. For example, in normal writing, letters from similar alphabets can be substituted to spell a word to facilitate translation. Yet, if the same were done with runes, the result would be a word that is meaningless or inadequately translatable. The fundamental alteration that occurs when one chooses to write with runes is that the language is phonetic in nature. Consequently, when constructing words, it is necessary to represent their sounds rather than their written form. Consider the example of writing the English word "Sing." The sound "S" is denoted by the rune Sowilo, followed by representing the sound "I" with Isa, and finally, the sound "NG" is represented by a single rune, Ingwaz, instead of using separate runes for "N" and "G." Therefore, the final rendering of the word in runes would be pronounced as "Sowilo Isa Ingwaz." Although this example is relatively simple, problems arise when trying to spell more complex words with runes. The main obstacle lies in the changes that have occurred in the language over time. The sounds used today differ from those used centuries ago, consequently posing difficulties in transcribing modern letters into runes. To begin the transcription process, it is first necessary to write the word in English, or the desired language. Ultimately, the word must be transformed into its phonetic form, and then assigned the corresponding rune for each letter or sound in the chosen language.

This guide will help you understand the letters and sounds well

1. Fehu symbolizes the letter F, as pronounced in the word fish.
2. Uruz symbolizes the letter U, as pronounced the double OO in the word stool.
3. Thurisaz symbolizes the letter TH, as pronounced in the word thorn.
4. Ansuz symbolizes the letter A, as pronounced in the word apple.

5. Raido symbolizes the letter R, as pronounced in the word radio.
6. Kauno symbolizes a "hard" C or K, as the C in clock and the K in the word key.
7. Gebo symbolizes the letter G, as pronounced in the word grape.
8. Wunjo symbolizes the letters W and V, as W sounds in wind and V in viper.
9. Hagalaz symbolizes the letter H, as pronounced in happy.
10. Naudiz represents the letter N, as pronounced in the word new.
11. Isa symbolizes the letter I, as pronounced in sing.
12. Jera represents the letters J and Y, as J pronounced in joke and Y in yak.
13. Ihwaz symbolizes the letters I and Y, as I pronounced in silo and Y pronounced in style.
14. Perth symbolizes the letter P, as pronounced in the word pork.
15. Algiz represents the letter Z, as pronounced in the word zebra. It can also represent the letter S, as in the word cousin.
16. Sowilo represents letter S or a C, as C sounds in lice and S sounds in see.
17. Tiwaz symbolizes letter T, as in the word tree.
18. Berkanan symbolizes letter B, as pronounced in the word bail.
19. Ehwaz symbolizes the letter E, as pronounced in the word elk.

20. Mannaz symbolizes the letter M, as pronounced in the word mail.
21. Laguz symbolizes the letter L, as pronounced in the word lawn.
22. Ingwaz symbolizes the letter NG, as a compound consonant ng, as pronounced in the word linger.
23. Othila symbolizes the letter O, as pronounced in the word orange.
24. Dagaz symbolizes the letter D, as pronounced in the word doll.

There are some guidelines that should be considered when venturing to write with runes. First, it should be noted that there are only 24 runes, as opposed to the 26 letters in the English alphabet. In addition, some letters in English are silent and do not contribute to the pronunciation of words. These letters should be ignored or omitted when transcribing words in runes. In ancient runic writing, spaces were not used and punctuation marks did not separate runes. However, in modern usage, some spaces are used to facilitate word separation. When writing with runes, it is also important to consider the direction in which the words are written. For optimal readability, it is recommended to write from left to right, reflecting the modern Western writing style. It is worth noting that in ancient texts writing could be done in both directions, adding an intriguing aspect to the interpretation of messages.

13
LAYOUT FOR READING

The practice of casting runes can be called either "layout" or "spread." Layout is the more classical way of casting, while spread is more akin to a tarot card reading. Although there may be slight variations in the techniques and interpretations adopted, the basic purpose remains the same: to gain insight, guidance and clarity from the runes. From my personal experience, the divergence between these two methods is negligible, and in the end it is a matter of selecting the one that aligns best with your personal preferences. Given their striking similarities, we will now delve into the one at hand and examine the various patterns (Layouts) in full.

ONE-RUNE LAYOUT

To achieve success in readings, it is essential to start with a clear and focused mind, and this attitude must be maintained for every throw. The first type of layout is known as a ***one-rune layout***. To begin, you need to bring out the thoughts or problems that are bothering you and focus exclusively on them. To receive guidance and help in resolving these issues, it is imperative to focus exclusively on this particular problem, then clear your mind, and "freeze" any other thoughts. To perform a single reading, draw a rune from the bag containing all the runes, or you can cast them and choose a single tile after casting on the cloth. Whichever method you choose, this rune will symbolize the attitude to be taken associated with the question for which guidance or resolution is sought. It can also be interpreted as the answer to that question. Although the answer may be broad and general in nature, as only one rune is read, it is essential to remain patient and understand what the runes want to communicate to us. Engaging in further casting or looking for a broader layout will only serve to confuse the ideas, making it much more difficult to determine whether the information received is correct. One must keep in mind that deeper and more accurate insights will emerge over time. As in all things, have patience and perseverance.

TWO-RUNE LAYOUT

This second layout adds a second rune, and although it may seem elementary, for beginners it is more than enough reading. Germanic peoples divided time into two distinct parts: the present and the future. That is why the arrangement of the ***two runes*** is particularly suited to this concept. Although the past plays a role in the arrangement of the three runes, for now it is not essential. When you cast your runes, the first one you select will relate to the present, providing insights, perspectives and solutions relevant to your present circumstances. The second rune will represent what has yet to happen, helping you make decisions for the future. It is important to trust your intuition when deciphering the meanings of the runes, as they have specific meaning for your life force. Even if you use only two runes and do not have one for the past, the first rune will still have traces of previous influences that will accompany the present moment. Rest assured that two runes are more than enough for a beginner, so take your time and wait patiently for the answers to arrive.

THREE-RUNE LAYOUT (PAST, PRESENT, AND FUTURE)

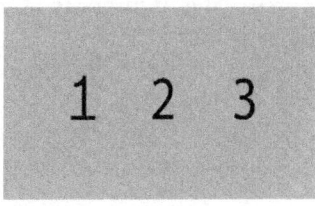

Some practitioners find the two-rune system deficient, believing that there should be at least enough runes to cover the various aspects of time. This is a matter of purely personal choice. With the ***three-rune layout***, we now have a complete view of the past, present and future.

The initial rune you cast (or select, if several are cast at the same time) will be located on the left side and will symbolize the past. It will reveal the decisions and choices that influenced the question you asked. This will allow you to gain information from past mistakes and prevent them from being repeated. The second rune, placed in the center, will represent your current circumstances. This may prove more challenging, as it will help you recognize the actions and emotions that currently influence or give rise to the problem under consideration. Recognizing that our own words or actions may be causing us distress or anxiety can be difficult to accept, but once we understand these factors, we can at least begin to address them. That leaves the third rune, to be placed on the right side, and it will reveal the outcome of our investigation. Analyzing the launch will enable you not only to discern the steps needed to change the current situation, but also to grasp the recommended approach and attitude for embarking on a journey of enlightenment and conscientious divination in the future.

LAYOUT OF THE FOUR DIRECTIONS

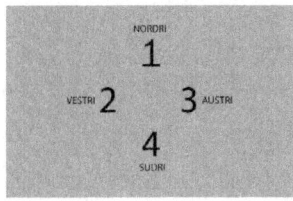

According to Norse mythology, the immense skull of Ymir is believed to be supported in the sky by four dwarves known as Nordri, Sudri, Austri and Vestri. This skull is considered the heavenly realm and is of significant importance. The strategic positioning of these dwarves aligns with the cardinal directions, which further emphasizes their power. When casting runes, the *"four-direction layout"* is oriented in the sequence north, south, east, west, thus avoiding any confusion. However, unlike the arrangements addressed before, there is the inclusion of an additional rune that follows the concept of time as we understand it. In this new arrangement, north, or Nordri, symbolizes the past. Recognizing what has gone before is essential, even though we may be reluctant to reflect on past mistakes or painful memories. This reflection is essential for development in rune reading and personal growth. The present is represented by the West, or Vestri. Questions asked and answers sought during divination are strongly influenced by the present moment. It is important to remember that Ancient Futhark aims to manifest positive energies in our lives, so any negativity encountered will be fleeting and, in the end, positivity will prevail. East, or Austri, does not exclusively predict future events, as the third rune typically does in the previous arrangement. Instead, it helps to identify potential obstacles and challenges that may arise along the path of life. Although different emotions may arise, they will all be related to the specific question posed, so there is no need to be overwhelmed. South, or Sudri, acts as a merger of the other three runes and can be considered the rune of the "future." It will guide us in the right direction and provide information about potential solutions when facing difficulties. When switching to layouts with more than three runes, it is common to experience some irregularities. This is inevitable with a larger number of runes, as the probability of such occurrences increases. However, these more complex combinations are in line with our growing experience. When we encounter a rune that seems incongruent with the rest of the reading, it is important to broaden our perspective and consider the reading as a whole. These skills develop over time, and it is when we do not exert excessive effort that readings become easier to interpret. Seeking accurate answers, keeping an open mind, and placing trust in the energies of the Ancient Futhark is crucial. In this way, the process of divination and interpretation of readings becomes significantly more manageable and easier.

FIVE-RUNE CROSS LAYOUT

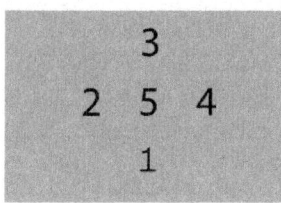

Five-rune layout, also known as *"cross layout"*, involves selecting five runes and placing them in the shape of a plus sign on the throwing cloth. In this rune reading practice, the approach you take will greatly influence the outcome, regardless of the number of runes used. Multiple runes may bring mixed answers, but the final result will always depend on your determination and application. Mix the runes in the bag with your right hand, draw out five runes with your left hand, and arrange them according to the pattern and sequence of numbers. The first rune placed ***on the right (4),*** symbolizes the past or root cause of the problem. The second Rune positioned ***to the left (2),*** reveals the current energies employed in the present. The third Rune is positioned ***downward (1),*** and offers a glimpse of the potential future if no action is taken. The fourth Rune is positioned ***upward (3),*** signifying the challenge that must be faced and overcome to change the future predicted by the third rune. The fifth Rune, located ***in the middle (5),*** indicates the energies and decisions, which should be sought primarily within ourselves, to improve the situation indicated by the third Rune. This method of reading illuminates a possible future based on passive actions. Ultimately, the future lies solely in our hands and in our dedication to improving circumstances. Neglecting the given advice and acting independently could even lead to a worse outcome than predicted by the third Rune. To extract Runes in this way, it is essential to have a clear intention in mind and focus on it carefully.

MIDGARD SERPENT LAYOUT

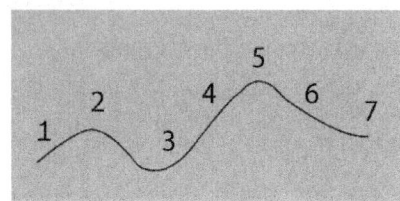

This layout is inspired by the mythical ***serpent Jormugandr***. Norse legends tell of Jormugandr's immense size, capable of encircling the earth and biting its own tail. This symbolism underscores the importance of attention when interpreting these runes, as their meaning can easily escape attention. In a fluid arrangement, the seven runes will line up as if embarking on a journey along the great serpent of ***Midgard***. Along the way, there are occasional uphill sections where obstacles may occur that impede progression. However, it is critical to recognize the presence of downhill stretches, which provide respite and an opportunity to gather strength before impending conflicts. Here is how to interpret the various arrangements of the runes.

1) The emblem embodies feelings of yesteryear and their intricate intertwining with the difficult situation for which you seek solace. Could you have taken some action that hastened the onset of this circumstance? Think carefully about this question.

2) It symbolizes the hardships you face because of the emotions encountered in the initial state. The hump embodies obstacles overcome and choices made to deal with previous circumstances, as they may prove beneficial in the present.

3) It is a particular juncture that symbolizes the intricate set of emotions surrounding your present situation. It has the greatest significance of the present, as it accurately reflects your present circumstances.

4) This is the crucial point from which you begin the journey toward your coveted goal. The challenges encountered in the previous stages may resurface, but the obstacle at this juncture is considerably greater than the one before. This means that the obstacles you will face will be challenging. However, you are now equipped with the wisdom gathered from past experiences, which will serve as a guiding light.

5) This represents the culmination of your journey, offering a glimpse of your final destination. This rune will clarify the intricate interplay between your emotions and their potential to influence your actions, particularly when you perceive that your goal is within reach.

6) The position serves as a reminder that there is still work to be done to achieve your desired goal. It is imperative to pay special attention to this rune. If it advises more effort, it is essential to adhere to its guidelines. For example, when encountering a rune of authority and dominion, it is necessary to show determination and regulate one's emotions until the desired goals are achieved.

7) It is the head of the Midgard Serpent, which represents for many the emblem of success, the ultimate goal. However, according to the tradition of Norse mythology, Jormugandr possesses the peculiar ability to bite its own tail. Therefore, one must pay diligent attention to the guidance of the ancient runes to avoid being trapped once again by the serpent's coils.

BIFROST LAYOUT

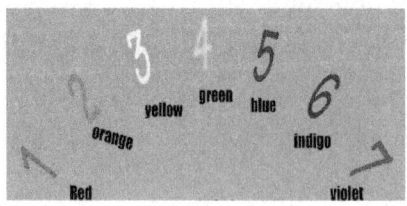

According to Norse mythology, ***the Bifrost*** is a celestial bridge resembling a rainbow that serves as a divine conduit between Midgard, the realm of humans, and Asgard, the realm of gods. Using this reading pattern, one will experience the feeling of receiving assistance and direction from divine entities. A sequence of seven runes is plotted and methodically arranged in a curved formation, beginning from the left with the color red, and ending with the color purple at its end.

Here is a simplified explanation of how to understand the various arrangements of the runes.

- **Red** - Includes your previous thoughts and behaviors that might affect the reading.

- **Orange** - This rune symbolizes the repercussions brought on by your previous mindset.

- **Yellow** - Symbolizes your past attitude that may have an effect on your initial application to the reading.

- **Green** - Symbolizes the impact of your current behavior on the final outcome.

- **Blue** - This rune represents the attitude you must have in the future.

- **Indigo** - It represents the effects in the future of the decisions you will make.

- **Purple** - It is the complete result of your inner journey. The Bifrost layout might seem complex, but if you examine it closely, it is only indications inherent in the past, present and future, with a couple of exceptions.

GRID OF NINE LAYOUT

```
4 9 2
3 5 7
8 1 6
```

The layout *"Grid of Nine"* involves casting nine runes and arranging them in a grid, like the diagram in the image. Be sure to adhere to the numbering provided, as it is of significant importance in improving the effectiveness of your reading. The uniqueness of this grid lies in the fact that by adding up the values of any row, column or even diagonal, the result will be consistently 15.

- To understand this pattern, start with the lowest horizontal row, which represents the factors that influenced the past.

8 ...*Includes hidden influences that occurred in the past.*

1 ....*Represents the basic influences you have experienced.*

6 ....*Represents current attitudes toward past events.*

The middle row from left to right, which includes:

3 ....*Represents the hidden influences acting in the present.*

5 ....*Represents the present condition.*

7 ....Represents your attitude toward events occurring in the present.

Finally we have the top row:

4 .....It refers to the obstacles that prevent you from emerging.

9 .....It is the absolute best answer to your initial question.

2 .....Indicates how you will act on the final outcome of the reading.

ODIN'S NINE LAYOUT

```
      4              9
 2        6          8
      3        5
 1              7
```

This layout is in reference to Odin, the Almighty, who according to Norse legend, hung on the branches of Yggdrasil to acquire the knowledge of runes. In the **Odin's nine Layout**, the first six runes precisely represent Odin (1 and 2 represent the legs and 4 represents the head), while the last three symbolize Odin's spear. To interpret this arrangement, follow the diagram below.

The runes in the first column (1 and 2) represent the elements of the past cause of your request.

1 ....Symbolizes the hidden factors that happened in the past.

2 ....*Represents actions taken with respect to the past.*

The column that includes runes 3 and 4 represents the actions that will lead to change.

3 ....*It includes the hidden factors currently occurring.*

4 ....*It is the attitude taken toward current events.*

The column with runes 5 and 6 depicts the answer to the question.

5 ....*This rune symbolizes the hidden influences, the delaying causes that may prevent the answer from manifesting.*

6 ....*Represents the actions that will be taken by the questioner in the future.*

The last column *(7, 8, and 9)* represents the powers at your disposal and the actions you must handle for the first, second, and third columns.

CELTIC CROSS SPREAD

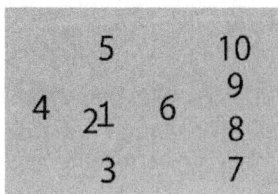

Although the *"Celtic cross"* spread is used for reading tarot cards, you can also use it for reading runes. After mixing the runes in the bag, you will have to cast 10 of them and arrange them following the numbering and layout of the image. Before casting, it is imperative to direct your attention to the rune you are asking for help. For example, if your intention is to achieve conception, select a rune that symbolizes fertility. Devote your concentration to this rune as you proceed to cast the ten tiles required for this arrangement. Place rune number 2 in an elevated position relative to rune number 1.

For a thorough understanding of this rune arrangement, here is how to read it:

1 ....Represents the question you are asking to be answered.

2 ....Symbolizes the obstacles that may arise.

3 ....Indicates influences that could change future events.

4 ....Includes influences you are going through or near the end.

5 ....Indicates influences that could become important.

6 ....Represents influences that you may encounter soon.

7 ....Includes present fears and negative thoughts.

8 ....Indicates outside influences that could potentially affect the outcome.

9 ....It refers to your beliefs and hopes.

10 ...The rune that offers the best outcome to your request.

This layout may seem a bit complicated, but you will have a complete and detailed picture of the situation.

EGIL'S WHALEBONE LAYOUT

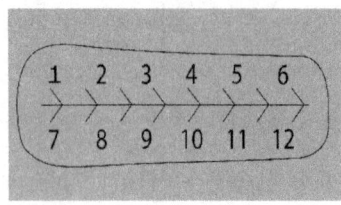

This layout takes inspiration from the famous Icelandic saga, *"Egil's Saga"*, which tells of the extraordinary exploits of a master poet and warrior named Egil. Within this epic tale, there is a chapter in which Egil miraculously heals Helga, Thorfinn's daughter, from an incurable illness. It is revealed that Helga's afflicted state is caused by the misplacement of runes on her head. Through his profound knowledge and skill, Egil removes the improper runes and skillfully replaces them with those newly engraved on a whale bone, immediately restoring the health of Thorfinn's daughter. Given the extraordinary complexity from the other readings, this scheme requires a unique approach. Instead of assigning individual meanings to each rune, groups of three runes are formed, allowing each trio to convey a unique message. Although familiarity with the saga is not a prerequisite for using this arrangement, possessing knowledge of its historical context can help to understand and retain the meaning of each group.

INTENTIONS OF THE CARVER (1, 2 AND 3)

Within the narrative, the rune carver possessed specific intentions for the runes. If you wish to seek advice from the runes, it is imperative that you think diligently about the answers you wish them to reveal. Be aware of this purpose as you meticulously select the runes you intend to use. It is of utmost importance to keep this intention at the forefront of your mind as you advance toward achieving the solution.

HELGA'S RESULTS (4, 5 AND 6).

Helga is damaged by the wandering runes placed on her forehead. This trio of runes possesses the power to reveal the sad consequences that would occur should you harbor impure motives or should you lack the commitment to achieve the desired outcome.

THORFINN'S WORRIES (7, 8 AND 9)

In the saga, the protagonist Thorfinn is worried about his ailing daughter, Helga, who lies on her deathbed. This group of runes represent the myriad external concerns one encounters while pursuing one's aspirations. These external influences possess the ability to help or disrupt progress in achieving the desired goal. For example, if the ultimate goal is to achieve financial stability, these external influences may manifest themselves in the form of assistance in difficult times or help in the search for a more secure and better-paid job opportunity. Ultimately, external forces can have a negative effect and either hinder the achievement of your goals or facilitate success. This set of runes will provide you with clues to potential dangers or helpful situations. It is your responsibility to figure out whether they will be beneficial or harmful.

EGIL'S RESULTS (10, 11 AND 12)

In the uplifting conclusion of this tale, it is Egil who takes center stage. Despite Helga's worrying state and Thorfinn's deep concern for his daughter, Egil skillfully uses his command over the runes to correct the chaos caused by the previous rune maker, thus restoring Helga to good health. However, this does not imply that one must constantly recast the runes until the desired result is achieved. Ultimately, the final set of three runes confers wisdom in overcoming the lessons of the past to achieve one's goals. However, it is crucial not to overlook the significance of the previous three sets, as they serve as warnings about the obstacles one may find on one's journey. These insights enable people to prepare for the challenges they may encounter.

What is intriguing about reading runes is the freedom to choose between adhering to the conventional approach (using one, two, three or four runes) or following more complex arrangements. Should one opt for the latter, it is imperative that the choice be dictated by personal inspiration. Above all, it remains crucial to rely on intuition to decipher the messages the runes want to communicate and of the potential interpretations suggested by the runes themselves.

14
COSMOLOGY AND NUMEROLOGY

COSMOLOGY

Ancient Norse civilizations saw the cosmos as more than just the Earth surrounded by the sky and the underworld. According to the Asatru belief system, the cosmos was a complex system of interconnected realms and planes. The narrative of the poem Völuspá recounts the events that occurred during the formation of the universe. The Norse cosmology is an engaging and intricate structure that reveals the interconnectedness of various worlds, reflecting the complex worldview of ancient Norse culture. At the center is Midgard, the realm of humans, surrounded by a vast ocean that serves as the boundary between human reality and the divine realms. Asgard, the majestic abode of the gods, dominates Midgard and is ruled by the all-powerful Odin, the god of wisdom and war. Within Asgard reside such deities including Thor, the god of thunder, and Frigg, the queen mother of the gods, each of whom plays a specific role in maintaining cosmic balance. Hel, located below Midgard, is a mysterious realm where the dead reside under the rule of the goddess Hel. As opposed to being a place of eternal punishment, Hel serves as a gateway to a future destiny, particularly for those who have not earned eternal glory through a heroic death in battle. Other worlds such as Alfheim, the realm of the light elves, and Svartalfheim, the realm of the dark elves or dwarves, exist along the branches of Yggdrasill, the tree of life. Each world contributes its own unique characteristics to the richness and complexity of Norse cosmology. The Norse conception of the cosmos is deeply rooted in a cyclical understanding of existence, symbolized by Ragnarök, the ultimate fate of the gods. This cataclysmic event causes the epic destruction of the cosmos, but also holds the potential for a new age and rebirth from the remnants of the old world. Ultimately, Norse cosmology offers a profound perspective on the interconnectedness of the gods and the cosmos, emphasizing the cyclical nature of life, death, and rebirth as integral components of a vast and intricate divine plan.

Here are some useful insights:

ALFHEIM

Alfheim, which translates to "the abode of the elves," serves as the realm of the elves. Positioned at the highest level of Yggdrasil, next to Asgard and Vanaheim, the domains of the Aesir and Vanir, Alfheim houses the palace of Freyr, ruler and deity. Despite the limited information available on the elves, who generally refrain from involvement in the events of

Norse mythology, it is widely acknowledged that the light elves, known as Ljosalfar, possess an unparalleled beauty that surpasses that of the sun and are revered as guardian angels. Endowed with magical abilities related to nature and fertility, they possess the ability to assist or harm humans. In contrast, the Dokkalfar, or dark elves, reside in Svartalfheim.

ÁSGARÐR

Ásgarðr was the ancestral land of the Æsir, a dominant pantheon consisting of Óðinn, Thórr and Frigg. According to Sturluson, Ásgarðr was an extremely fertile land in which vast riches, precious gems and gold were bestowed. The kingdom was surrounded by an incomplete wall, the construction of which was offered by a skilled stonemason in exchange for the hand of the goddess Freyja in marriage, as well as possession of the sun and moon. This proposal was accepted by the gods, unaware that the stonemason was actually a masked giant of Hrimthurs. After discovering this deception, Thórr quickly delivered a fatal blow to the stonemason, leaving the wall unfinished. In addition, Ásgarðr serves as the home of Valhalla, the great hall where Óðinn presides. Inside Valhalla, fallen warriors who died in battle, known as Einherjar, participate in lavish feasts and prepare to assist the gods during Ragnarök.

JÖTUNHEIMR

Jötunheimr is recognized as the realm of the giants (Jötnar). It is located far from Asgard, near the river Ífingr, and is believed to have been under the second root of Yggdrasil, where Ginnungagap existed. Útgarðar (also known as Utgard) is the main city of Jötunheimr and serves as a fortified refuge for the giants. The kingdom is ruled by Útgarða-Loki (also identified as Skrýmir). Descriptions portray the realm as perpetually frozen and shrouded in the frost of winter, characterized by dense forests and towering mountains. It is within Jötunheimr, where Óðinn sacrificed one of his eyes, to gain wisdom at the well of Mímisbrunnr.

HELHEIM

According to Norse mythology, Hel is considered one of the nine worlds in Scandinavian cosmology in which the dead reside. It is recognized as the abode of Hel, the queen of the dead, and is commonly referred to as Helheimr. Hel possesses the authority to assign dwellings to the dead, usually those who have died due to disease or old age. Hel is considered extremely prosperous, with majestic walls and gates adorning her realm. This domain served as an afterlife for individuals who had not experienced a meaningful or heroic death, or whom the gods deemed not brave enough to join them in the final battle of Ragnarök. In contrast to the Christian concept of "hell," the Norse afterlife represented more a continuation of existence in another realm rather than a realm of eternal torment.

MIDGARD

Midgard serves as the earthly realm, also known as the world of humans, located at the base of Yggdrasil and serves as a link to the other nine realms. Not only is Midgard located at the center of these realms, but it also incorporates elements of both order and chaos, resembling a combination of Innangard and Utahngard. Moreover, Midgard is positioned between Asgard and Hel, and these three realms are not only linearly connected on Yggdrasil but also intertwined. Asgard and Midgard are connected by the Bifrost, a vibrant rainbow bridge that ends at Himinbjorg, the abode of the deity Heimdall. Similarly, Hel is accessible through tombs leading to the underworld.

MUSPELHEIM

Muspelheim, the initial realm that arose from Ginnungagap, manifested as a realm shrouded in relentless fire. It served as the abode of the formidable fire giants under the rule of Surtr, the foreboding fire destined to engulf the world in Ragnarök. As expounded in Gylfaginning within the "Prose Edda," it is foretold that the burning fire giants of Muspelheim will devastate the majestic Bifröst Bridge during the catastrophic event of Ragnarök.

NIFLHEIM

Niflheim can be loosely translated as "Residence of the Mist." Within various texts, Niflheim's role often overlaps with that of Hel, suggesting that as a result of her involvement in the creation of the world, the realm became the designated home of the queen of the underworld. Niflheimr, the second world to form, was an icy realm that was home to the well of Hvergelmir, from which all of Élivágar's glacial streams and rivers originate. According to the Prose Edda, Niflheim predates the creation of Midgard and contained a cave known as Hvergelmir, which served as the source of several toxic rivers called Élivágar.

The names of the rivers were *Svol, Gunnthro, Forma, Finbul, Thul, Slid and Hrid, Sylg and Ylg, Vid, Leipt and Gjoll.*

NIÐAVELLIR

Another Norse kingdom that was home to mythical creatures is Niðavellir, where a race of enigmatic and industrious beings known as dwarves thrived in the depths. Their subterranean realm, built mostly of stone, was veiled in secrets and bore the Old Norse name of "moonset" or "new moon." This mystical domain, also called Svartalfheim, evoked an aura of darkness and frost, lit only by the flickering flashlights lining its high walls and the unceasing fires burning in its forges. The waves of smoke that permeated the air were harmoniously intertwined with the gloomy essence of the realm. Within this realm, talented craftsmen tirelessly created extraordinary treasures, many of which have great significance in Norse mythology. Among their extraordinary creations are Thor's mighty hammer, Mjolnir, and Odin's formidable spear, Gungnir. It is also widely believed that the dwarves of Nidavellir were the masterminds behind the enchanting magic ring, Draupnir.

VANAHEIM

Vanaheim, home kingdom of the Vanir, is located west of Asaheim. The Vanir were renowned for their wisdom, fertility and prophetic abilities. However, following their clash with the Æsir, the Vanir joined this divine group. In the Heimskringla, Vanaheim is described as being located around the Don River (which was once known as the "Fork of Vana"). In addition, it is the realm in which the deity Njǎrðr was raised.

NUMEROLOGY

Numerology and Norse mythology are two fascinating areas that, although they come from different cultural traditions, can converge in interesting ways.

Numerology involves the interpretation of the symbolic meanings of numbers, while Norse history is full of tales and symbols associated with the gods and mythical creatures of mythology. When combined, these fields create a captivating context for exploration and reflection. Many ancient cultures ascribed deep meanings to numbers and often associated them with spiritual forces. Numerology refers to numbers as single digits, but in some areas, they have specific and mystical meanings. In fact, the interpretation of numbers in numerology, varies according to cultural and symbolic context. In the Norse context, it is possible to explore the meanings of some key numbers. Significant is the number 9, which reflects the importance of cycles in Norse mythology. The Norse cosmos consists of nine worlds, each inhabited by different gods, creatures and entities. The number 9 is often associated with completeness and perfection, symbolizing the interconnectedness of all elements within the grand scheme of the world. This can be interpreted as reflecting the nine interconnected worlds of Norse mythology, each with its own destiny. The number 3, often recurring in Norse narratives, can be interpreted as representing the tripartite cycles of creation, destruction and rebirth. In addition, the number 3 represents the trio of those primarily responsible for the creation of the world: Odin, the powerful ruler of the gods; Vili, associated with willpower and strength; and Vé, who symbolizes the sacred and mysterious. This triad forms the foundation of the Norse cosmos, underscoring the great significance of the number 3 in Norse beliefs.

The connection between numerology and Norse mythology becomes especially fascinating when examining the analysis of time cycles, especially through the events of Ragnarök, the ultimate fate of the gods. This significant event, rich in symbolism, represents not only a catastrophe but also an opportunity for renewal and rebirth. Even such a fundamental element as the runes, add another layer of numerical and symbolic meaning. Each rune corresponds to a sound, a concept and a number. Incorporating runes into numerological practice further enhances the understanding of hidden meanings, bridging the gap between scripture and Norse spirituality.

In conclusion, the integration of numerology and Norse mythology offers a unique and profound approach to exploring spirituality. This fusion of ancient traditions provides a fertile space for personal reflection, enabling anyone who immerses themselves in this union to discover deeper meanings about the nature of existence and the inherent order of the Norse world.

15
THE POEMS OF THE GODS

THE EDDAS

The Eddas, a pair of medieval Icelandic manuscripts, contain a rich set of prose and poetry that delves into the mythology, religion, and history of ancient Scandinavian society. Composed of poems of the eddic or skaldic genre, they use alliterative verse and symbolism to captivate the reader. Although the precise origin of the term "Edda" remains elusive, one plausible explanation points to the Old Norse word "óðr," meaning "poetry." These priceless collections, called the Poetic Edda and Prose Edda, offer profound insight into the Norse cultural heritage.

POETIC EDDA

This esteemed tome delves into the realm of Norse mythology through a collection of captivating poems. The main sources of information within the Poetic Edda are two notable compositions, "Völuspá," meaning "The Seer's Insight," and "Grímnismál," meaning "The Song of the

Hooded One." Of these, "Völuspá" is the most informative, as it recounts a fascinating encounter between Odin, the venerable ruler of the gods, and a wise woman whom he asks to foretell the future. Surprisingly, despite not knowing Odin's story, it reveals the origins of the cosmos, the birthplaces of the first dwarves, elves and humans. Although understanding the complexities of the poetic Edda may prove challenging in contemporary times, it resonated perfectly with those who once worshiped Norse deities. Originating in the 13th century, the Old Edda, also known as the Poetic Edda, emerged as a collection of Icelandic and Norse sagas meticulously preserved within the illustrious Codex Regius, or the "Royal Book." Over time, numerous other poems were incorporated into the Poetic Edda, each meticulously composed with visionary fervor and brilliance. This masterpiece follows these four rules:

- *The author is anonymous.*
- *He takes a direct approach to word order.*
- *He uses a certain metric (fornyröislag, ljóðaháttr and málaháttr).*
- *The kenné (ancient rhetorical figures) are used less.*

The Poetic Edda is surely the most extensive source on Norse mythology. It consists of two parts: the Mythological Poems and the Heroic Tales. The Mythological Poems recounts the adventures of the gods from their point of view and includes eleven poems: Völuspá, Hávamál, Vafþrúðnismál,

Grimnismál, Skirnismál, Hábarðsljóð, Hymiskviða, Lokasenna, Þrymskviða, Völundarkviða and Alvíssmál. The Heroic Songs, divided into three parts, describes the challenges and journeys of heroes and heroines and contains nineteen songs:

1. The Helgi Lays consist of six stories: Helgakviða Hundingsbana I, Helgakviða Hjörvarðssonar, Helgakviða Hundingsbana II, Helgakviða Hundingsbana I, Helgakviða Hjörvarðssonar, and Helgakviða Hundingsbana II.

2. The Niflung Cycle consists of fifteen short stories: Frá dauða Sinfjötla, Grípisspá, Reginsmál, Fáfnismál, Sigrdrífumál, Brot af Sigurðarkviðu, Guðrúnarkviða I, Sigurðarkviða hin skamma, Heimreið Brynhildar, Dráp Niflunga, Guðrúnarkviða II, Guðrúnarkviða III, Oddrúnargrátr, Atlakviða, and Atlamál hin grenienzku.

3. The Jörmunrekkr Lays, consisting of two stories: Guðrúnarhvöt, Hamðismál.

PROSE EDDA

Snorri Sturluson, a renowned Icelandic scholar, is the author of the Edda in Prose, a significant literary work for the Norse. Snorri possessed a vast knowledge of Norse history and mythology, which is evident in his book. Although the Prose Edda includes several poems and information from the Poetic Edda, Snorri also introduced new material. Some of the poems in the prose Edda were borrowed from ancient sources now lost. However, it is important to note that not all of Snorri's writings can be considered real, as he occasionally invented details and modified narratives. Therefore, it is crucial to approach some texts with caution, as the authors had the freedom to manipulate events and present their own interpretations. Fortunately, scholars have been able to identify the parts of the stories invented by Snorri. In this book we will focus on the stories that Snorri did not alter. The first story you will encounter, derived from the poetic Edda, delves into the Norse creation myth, exploring the origins of the world. The Prose Edda, also known as the Young Edda, is an Icelandic textbook that dates back to the 13th century. It is widely believed that Snorri Sturluson played a significant role in its composition. Snorri's literary style, influenced by court poetry, elevated his status among his peers. The enigmatic nature of Snorri Sturluson has long puzzled scholars interested in the study of medieval Norse culture. It is only by reconciling the contradictions surrounding this famous figure that a complete understanding of Snorri and his work can be achieved (Wanner, 2008). It should be emphasized that the reinterpretation of these stories altered the features and influences of the deities in some writings, but also made them more accessible to readers.

The prose Edda was typically written in the skaldic poetic genre following these rules:

- *The author is known.*

- *Sentences are commonly interwoven and contain ornate syntax.*
- *Ornate meter (dróttkvætt or a variant thereof) is used.*
- *Quotations are frequently used.*

The prose Edda consists of four sections:

- *Prologue*
- *Gylfaginning*
- *Skáldskaparmál*
- *Háttatal*

MAGIC AND POETRY

Odin and Freya are esteemed shamans in the pantheon of Norse deities. Shamanism is a mystical practice in which individuals communicate with spirits and navigate the ethereal realm to achieve desired results. Odin is famous for his spiritual journeys, during which his body remained in Asgard, appearing to others as if he were asleep. A notable example is when he ventured into the underworld riding Sleipnir, an eight-legged steed associated with shamanic trance, to discover Baldur's fate. Being a practitioner of shamanism, Odin is surrounded by a multitude of animal spirits, including his ravens, the wolves Geri and Fleki, and even the Valkyries (although they are maidens, they too are spiritual entities serving Odin). The death and rebirth ritual Odin undergoes to unlock the mysteries of the runes is also an integral aspect of shamanic customs, and leaves no room for doubt about his supernatural ability. Shamanism is closely intertwined with traditional seidr, a form of magic traditionally thought to be suitable only for women—that is why Freya is its patroness. Men who engaged in seidr were despised and even ostracized by society; animosity ran deep. Odin's affinity for shamanism made him the target of ridicule and derision. His ten-year exile from Asgard is said to have been partly a consequence of his inclination toward "feminine" activities. To claim that magic marred Odin's reputation would be an immense understatement. It questioned his honor and his ability to fulfill his "manly" duties. However, for Odin, the concept of honor was not fundamental and he willingly discarded it if it meant being able to take part in contemplative practices. Odin's association with poetry dates back to the time when he stole the mead of poetry (mead of Suttungr), a mixture created by dwarves from the remains of Kvasir, the wisest man who ever lived. Drinking this drink conferred knowledge and the aptitude to compose verse. Naturally Odin coveted this elixir and came into possession of it by cunning, seducing the giantess in charge of its custody. However, in a show of magnanimity, Odin chose to share the gift of poetry with humans, gods and other entities, solidifying his status as the patron saint of scholars, poets, storytellers and composers. To show his poetic skill, Odin is said to communicate exclusively in verse.

RUNE POEMS

Runic poems serve as a primary source of information regarding the 16-letter alphabet of Young Futhark. These poems offer a poetic stanza for each runic letter, helping the user to retain pronunciation and meaning. Within these poems are remarkable verses that convey vivid imagery, aiding in the memorization of rune names. The poems are classified into three sections: poems on Norse runes, poems on Icelandic runes, and poems on Anglo-Saxon runes. The Norse and Icelandic poems are based on the Younger Futhark, while the Anglo-Saxon poems use the Anglo-Saxon runic alphabet. Considering the vast amount of information available on the various versions of these poems, the most organized version is considered, namely the Anglo-Saxon Runic Poem, "Linguarum veterum septentrionalium Thesaurus." Printed in London in 1705 by Hickes, it consists of 29 short rooms, of two to five lines each, preceded by descriptions of the runic characters and their names. It is derived, most likely, from an ancient Scandinavian poem.

CONCLUSIONS

Thank you for taking the time to read this book. Incorporating the reading of texts about the history of the ancient Norse people into your daily life can be an important aspect of your inner journey. Engaging in the Norse faith requires a certain level of preparation, so it is essential to make sure you are ready before embarking on this spiritual path. Norse rituals were deeply rooted in values that were meaningful to people. The act of making sacrifices, for example, instilled gratitude and prevented tribes from taking many things for granted. Through the offering of sacrifices, pagans also learned the transitory aspect of material goods, redirecting their attention to more important values, such as human or nature values. To truly harness the power of the runes, it is essential to have a complete understanding of their history and mythology. This knowledge is critical to deciphering their authentic and complete meaning. Although the history of runes can be traced back to the earliest forms of writing, it is important to recognize that some people associate them with magic. Many people believe that they possess a wide range of powers that can guide a person along the path of life. Undoubtedly, this book has broadened your horizons, captured your interest and introduced you to the fascinating and enigmatic Norse world. Now, it is your responsibility to interpret the signs of the afterlife when you read the runes and strive to direct your life toward a more fulfilling and less tortuous path. Good luck and always broaden your horizons!

Printed in Dunstable, United Kingdom